A Guide to

Texas Rivers and Streams

A Guide to
Texas Rivers and Streams

Gene Kirkley

Lone Star Books®
A Division of Gulf Publishing Company
Houston, Texas

Acknowledgments

I am indebted to and wish to thank the following agencies and individuals for their help in supplying the information, maps, and pictures that contributed to this book: the Texas Parks and Wildlife Department; U.S. Army Corps of Engineers; Bob Narramore and Ben Nolen; and Don Greene and friends at Whitewater Experience.

The maps were adapted from *An Analysis of Texas Waterways: A Report on the Physical Characteristics of Rivers, Streams, and Bayous in Texas;* prepared by the Texas Parks and Wildlife Department, 4200 Smith School Road, Austin, Texas; published by the Texas Agricultural Extension Service, the Texas A&M University System, College Station, Texas; with technical assistance from the River Recreation Association of Texas; based on an analysis of Texas waterways conducted by Harold J. Belisle and Ron Josselet; under the direction of Ron Thuma and Clayton T. Garrison.

A Guide to
Texas Rivers and Streams

Gulf Publishing Company
Book Division
P.O. Box 2608 □ Houston, Texas 77252-2608

Library of Congress Cataloging in Publication Data

Kirkley, Gene.
    A guide to Texas rivers and streams.

    1. Rivers—Texas—Recreational use—Guidebooks. 2. Rivers—Texas—Description. 3. Texas—Description and travel—1981—Guide-books. I. Title.
GV191.42.T4K57 1983   917.640463   83-12941
ISBN 0-88415-781-4

        10 9 8 7 6 5 4 3 2

Book Design by Pat Wiles

Contents

(Publisher's note: This is out of alphabetical order because the author wanted to save his favorite for last.)

Preface

The earliest records of man and the progress of civilization are very closely related to the rivers and streams of the world. From the most ancient time right up to the present day, rivers and streams have played an all-important role in everyone's life.

Civilization is said to have begun in the Tigris-Euphrates Valley; the valley of the Nile in Egypt was the site of a highly-developed civilization. As a means of transportation and a source of many of life's necessities, the value of a river is immeasurable, because it extends into every phase of our existence. Even today in Texas, rivers and streams play an important part in providing the good life that we have.

I had the privilege of growing up in East Texas when it was safe to drink from just about any flowing stream. We had never even heard of pollution like we have today. We just made sure that there wasn't a dead cow or something upstream, and since there weren't too many cow fatalities, we usually didn't bother to look.

Flowing through Dad's bottom pasture was a wet-weather stream that we simply called the "branch." During the hot, dry weather of late summer, it ceased to flow with only the deeper holes providing water for the cattle. Some of these never completely dried up, and they managed to keep enough water for the few catfish and bream to survive. My older brother and I spent lots of hours with a cane pole and a can of worms fishing up and down those banks.

If the spring of the year happened to be an exceptionally wet one, with an early flood or two, deep holes would be created in some of the sharper bends of the branch. One of these, no more than 15 feet across, we would turn into our private swimmin' hole. And that's where I first learned to swim without the aid of "cans." Kids nowadays probably never heard of "swimmin' cans," but they were commonplace back then for non-swimmers. To make them, you took a couple of empty syrup buckets, the gallon size, made sure the lids were on tight, and put them in a big feed sack. After sewing up the open end, you tied string around the sack between the buckets to hold one in each end. To use the contraption in the water, you just lay across it with your arms in front of the buckets. It was kind of awkward until you got used to it, but it sure worked!

I was reminded of the great fun we had along that little stream when I crossed a similar stream this past summer on a trip through the Texas Panhandle. By the time July rolls around, a great many of those creeks and rivers have slowed to just a trickle. On the map, this one was identified as a river, but the water in the wide sandy bed was no more than a foot across in places. Seated in and along the stream were several youngsters playing and having a ball while the old folks were enjoying a game of cards in the shade of a nearby mesquite.

I mention both of these instances to show that the opportunity for recreation on Texas rivers and streams is not limited to the biggest and best known. Sure, if you must use a big power boat as you speed up and down the waterway, select a major river during a period of adequate water flow. If your fun comes from running white-water rapids in either an inflatable raft, a canoe, or a kayak, you'll need to select a river that has that kind of water and go during the time when the flow is high, either after heavy rains or when the discharge from the reservoir upstream is at a peak.

One of the good things about Texas waterways is, unless you happen to be a "purist" with only one kind of water from which you get your "enjoys," there are always plenty of opportunities for outdoor recreation, year round. In the fall before the rains begin, with most of the rivers flowing at their low-water marks, there's nothing I enjoy more than to load my canoe with a camping outfit and float between bridges, spending the night on an exposed gravel or sand bar. This can be about the closest thing to a real wilderness experience that is still easily available. Most of us do not have either the time or the opportunity to travel the distance that might be required to really "get away from it all."

This guide will help you find many such float areas and will answer your questions about where to launch and take out. Please bear in mind however that the conditions on any given river or stream can change dramatically over a short period of time. To me, that is a part of the challenge and excitement of this part of our great outdoors. Most of our rivers can present entirely different situations with only a drop of a foot or two in the water level.

A couple of years or so ago a friend and I planned a canoe trip on an East Texas river during the month of October. The river flows for some 40 miles through prime hardwood bottomland abundant with wildlife.

Once considered an eyesore, the San Antonio River now offers a unique recreational opportunity in the midst of the city of San Antonio.

We left my car at our downstream takeout point, and his wife drove us around to our launch site. It was to be a leisurely float with two nights in camp. The fellow who recommended the trip had said that he had no trouble making it in two full days on the river. What he didn't tell me was that at the time he made it, the water level was considerably higher. We ran into trouble from the very start with downed trees that extended all the way across at the water line. To get by, we would run the canoe up on the log, he would climb out on the log and steady the canoe until I, too, could climb over all our gear to the log. Then we would pull the loaded canoe over where I could get back in and pick him up to move on down to the next log barring our progress.

There were so many of these that by the end of the second afternoon, we had traveled less than half of our intended float. Luckily, we found some people at a camp who carried me to where we had left my car for the takeout. In astronaut terms, we "aborted" that float the next morning. I have an idea that it would have taken us a full week to have covered the entire distance at that water level. And only once did we encounter a log jam that forced us to portage around it. The fellow who had recommended that float later assured me he had had no such problems. So it is always best to be prepared for something different from what you've been told. Even with the help of this guide which has been prepared from my own experience and the help of other sources listed in the acknowledgments, you can expect circumstances and conditions to change. Let me urge everyone who uses our waterways to be careful and observe *all* the rules of water safety. Too often we become complacent and think, "Oh, that will never happen to me!" But tragedies can, and will, happen when we don't use common sense.

Keep in mind that the use of Texas rivers and streams is increasing each year, and all of us have the obligation to do our part in what I call "stream keeping." Bring all your trash out with you. The old conservationists' advice "Take nothing but pictures and leave nothing but footprints" is still very good even though your footprints will be limited to that gravel or sand bar. And just because that beverage can or bottle will sink is no reason to litter the bottom either!

As you use these rivers and streams in Texas, it is my sincere wish that you will love and appreciate them as I do. The fellow that said "Texas has more rivers and less water" didn't know what he was talking about. Here's hoping that you will enjoy the recreational opportunities they offer.

How to Use This Guide

The rivers in this guide are arranged alphabetically so you can look up quickly and easily any river in which you are interested. A section on the secondary streams and rivers of Texas is included at the end of the book in case you don't find your favorite waterway listed in the first part.

While most of the rapids on Texas rivers will not give you any serious trouble, I have mentioned the "Class" of some of them. According to the International Scale of River Difficulty, rapids are rated as Class I through VI. Class I indicates a good current with some small waves and riffles with little or no obstructions. Class II rapids may have waves up to three feet with plenty of room through the channels that will require some maneuvering. Class III rapids are more difficult as they may have narrow channels through obstructions that call for more complex maneuvering. They can also have higher waves that are capable of swamping your canoe. Class IV should only be attempted by experienced canoeists as they are long, difficult, and possibly dangerous with very rough water. Always take a look from the shore, and plan in advance for a possible emergency. Covered canoes and kayaks are more suitable. Class V rapids are extremely difficult and hazardous requiring expert maneuvering with no room for mistakes! Advance scouting from the shore is essential. Rescue in case of mishap would also be very difficult. Class VI rapids are very dangerous and almost impossible to run in a canoe or even a kayak. These should be attempted only by experts working in teams and taking all precautions against accidents.

Keep in mind that the class of a rapid can change with a change in the water level brought on by either heavy rain in the upper watershed or by a variance in the amount of water released through a dam. Even the experienced person should always wear a Coast Guard approved personal flotation device when going through any rapid. All gear should be protected from both a wetting and possible loss in case of an upset. Stay with the canoe, but be sure to keep on the upstream side so as not to be pinned to a rock or other obstruction by the force of the current against the canoe. The pressure exerted can sometimes be measured in tons!

If you should find yourself afloat in swift water and away from your craft, be sure to keep your feet high and in front of you as you speed downstream as a protection against striking rocks or other objects. Some type of hard hat or helmet is recommended for added head protection for the more difficult floats.

Swimmers play in the spillway on the Guadalupe River near Seguin.

As you enjoy the recreational opportunities offered by the rivers and streams of Texas, be sure to keep in mind that most of the shorelines are private property. Here in Texas, roughly two percent of the land remains in public ownership. Of that total, about one-fifth is riverbed acreage. Although the adjacent land may be private property, most of the legally navigable watercourses are public property. And while the laws concerning the right of the public to use the stream banks are very ambiguous, the policy has been that the person who steps from his boat on a navigable river onto the bank above the midpoint of the high and low water line may be guilty of trespass. Since that is a point that is usually very difficult to identify, it can create a touchy situation. The trespass laws in Texas do have "teeth" in them, and a person can be charged with a misdemeanor offense even if there is no fence or posted signs. So not only do sand and gravel bars offer the best campsites, they may be the only spots where you can legally stop since they are considered below that midpoint of high and low water.

A word of caution: A sand or gravel bar on a river that is subject to fast changes in water flow due either to an upstream flood or release from a dam can be a very dangerous place to camp. More than a few campers have awakened to find themselves flooded. And that, my friend, is definitely not the way I like to wake up!

It is the purpose of this guide to serve as a help towards enjoying the recreational opportunities that are offered by the 80,000 miles of waterways in this great state. Within the past two decades, the building of large reservoirs has changed the character of many of Texas' rivers. In some instances, the restricted flow downstream has adversely affected their recreational use, but in others, the lowering of water temperature and the periods of high water during discharge have created an entirely new fishing and floating paradise!

The variety of waterways available here in Texas is tremendous. Ranging from the deep, slow-moving streams and bayous in the eastern portion of the state to the fast-flowing waters rushing through deep canyons in the southwest, the kind of action that you prefer is not likely to be too far away. It is hoped that this guide will enable you to find the river or stream that will offer you the kind of outdoor recreation you seek.

The scenic beauty of Texas rivers makes a float trip, for an afternoon or for a week, a most rewarding adventure.

Before You Launch

Included in this book are many different waterways—from the slow-moving, almost currentless bayous to the swift rapids of rock-filled rivers. I hope you will choose the type that matches your experience and ability. If you are a newcomer to either canoeing, kayaking, rafting, or just running the river in your bass boat, don't bite off more than you can chew, but learn as you go.

Space will not allow a lot of "how to" in this "where to" book, but a few basic tips will get you started in the right direction:

1. Wear a personal flotation device (life jacket) even if you are an accomplished swimmer.
2. Use waterproof bags and containers.
3. Carry an extra paddle—even for a day trip. (Losing one could put you in a bind.)
4. Wear a helmet or hard hat when running rapids. (Those rocks are much harder than your head. I know, I've hit a few of them.)
5. Be sure a responsible person knows where you are going and how long you plan to be gone. In the event of trouble, help will be on its way much sooner.
6. Tie everything down.
7. Distribute weight and gear evenly. Don't overload your craft. (If you have to do some portaging, you have to carry what you brought.)
8. Check out any water that looks hazardous before proceeding. Portage around any rapids that you have doubts about.
9. Carry an adequate first-aid and survival kit including sunburn protection, insect repellent, chapstick, snakebite kit, knife, and waterproof matches.
10. Learn about water danger signals such as hydraulics, pillows, strong currents, and strainers.
11. Never stand up in a canoe in moving water.
12. Dress adequately for the weather. (Carry rain gear.) Leave clean, dry clothing at the takeout point.
13. Take extra rope for lining (pulling) your canoe through rough water.
14. Carry a canoe repair kit.
15. Carry adequate drinking water.
16. Check water level of rivers before you start.
17. Carry all your trash out with you. Leave camping areas cleaner than you found them.

Here is some suggested reading that will help you learn the skills you need when you launch your chosen craft on one of the rivers and streams of Texas:

Basic River Canoeing by Robert E. McNair, American Camping Association, Inc., Bradford Woods, Martinsville, IN 46151

The Canoer's Bible by Robert D. Mead, Doubleday and Company, Inc.

Malo's Complete Guide to Canoeing and Canoe Camping by John Malo, Quadrangle Books of Chicago.

Texas Rivers and Rapids by Ben M. Nolen and R. E. Narramore, 12421 N. Central Expwy., Dallas.

Wilderness Canoeing by John Malo, The Macmillan Company, New York.

Wildwater Touring by Scott and Margaret Arighi, Macmillan Publishing Co., Inc., New York.

Handbooks on canoeing by the Boy Scouts of America and the American Red Cross.

Once you make your first launch, the chances are good that you will get "floatin' fever." I've not found a cure; you simply treat it by planning your next float! It's my hope that you come to love it as much as I do.

Major Texas Rivers

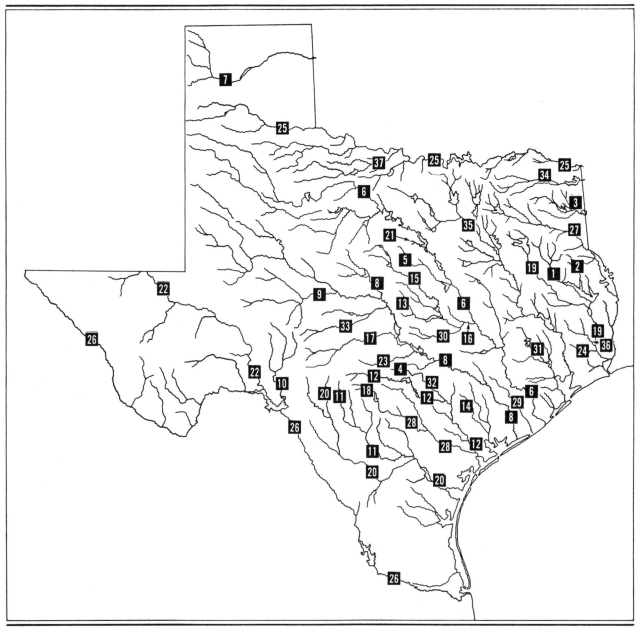

1. Angelina River	14. Lavaca River	27. Sabine River
2. Attoyac Bayou	15. Leon River	28. San Antonio River
3. Big Cypress Bayou	16. Little River	29. San Bernard River
4. Blanco River	17. Llano River	30. San Gabriel River
5. Bosque River	18. Medina River	31. San Jacinto River, West Fork
6. Brazos River	19. Neches River	32. San Marcos River
7. Canadian River	20. Nueces River	33. San Saba River
8. Colorado River	21. Paluxy River	34. Sulphur River
9. Concho River	22. Pecos River	35. Trinity River
10. Devil's River	23. Pedernales River	36. Village Creek
11. Frio River	24. Pine Island Bayou	37. Wichita River
12. Guadalupe River	25. Red River	
13. Lampasas River	26. Rio Grande	

MAJOR RIVERS AND WATERWAYS

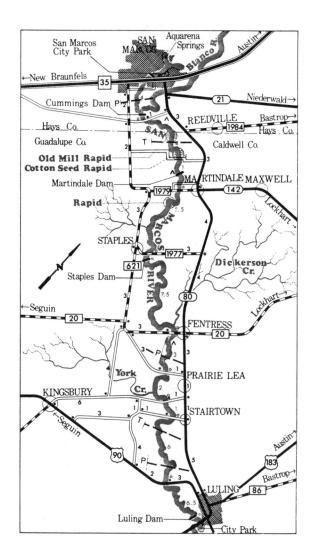

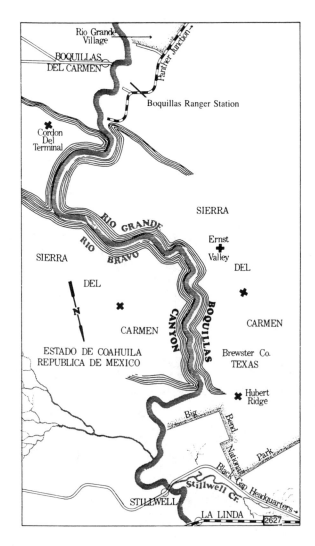

MAP KEY

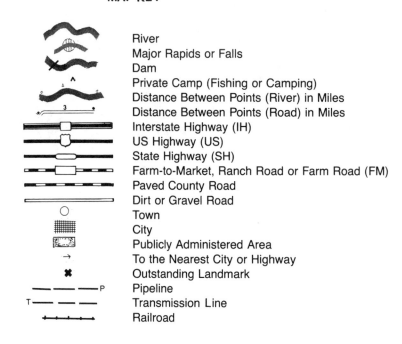

River
Major Rapids or Falls
Dam
Private Camp (Fishing or Camping)
Distance Between Points (River) in Miles
Distance Between Points (Road) in Miles
Interstate Highway (IH)
US Highway (US)
State Highway (SH)
Farm-to-Market, Ranch Road or Farm Road (FM)
Paved County Road
Dirt or Gravel Road
Town
City
Publicly Administered Area
To the Nearest City or Highway
Outstanding Landmark
Pipeline
Transmission Line
Railroad

Angelina River

Beginning with the junction of several creeks in Rusk County, the Angelina flows over 100 miles through pineywoods and hardwood bottomlands to its junction with the Neches near the upper end of Dam "B" or B. A. Steinhagen Reservoir. Some 20 miles upstream from this point is McGee Bend Dam that forms Sam Rayburn Reservoir. The river was named for Angelina (Little Angel), a Hainai Indian girl who was converted to Christianity and played an important role in the early development of this region.

There are several forest service and U.S. Corps of Engineers campgrounds and parks on Sam Rayburn Lake and in the Martin Dies, Jr. State Park on Dam "B" that offer excellent camping facilities for the outdoor recreationist.

Although it would be difficult to make a lengthy float on the upper reaches of the river due to log jams, drifts, and downed trees that extend the width of the stream, there are accessible portions that offer fun and fishing. There is a five-mile stretch from the US 84 crossing between Rusk and Mount Enterprise down to the SH 204 crossing west of Cushing. There is ample shoreline at both crossings for public use plus a roadside park at the SH 204 area. There is another crossing downstream of FM 343 with plenty of access area. This 16-mile portion may possibly be open enough for a float-through during periods of high water. The recreationist should always be prepared for delays and possible emergencies during this kind of float due to downed brush and log jams. The 17-mile stretch from here to the SH 21 crossing east of Alto passes through land owned by large timber companies. Some of these still allow public access through their property, but always get permission and specific instructions as to the location of access points to avoid the possibility of trespass. Log jams and drifts are likely here, too.

Perhaps the best bet for an extended float would be on that portion from SH 21 to SH 7 or on down

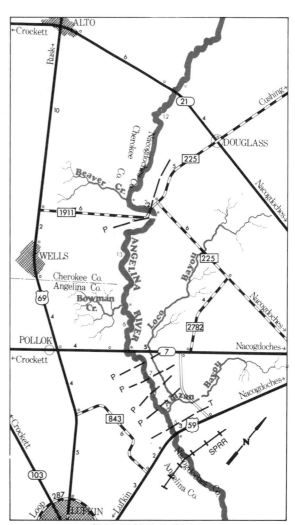

ANGELINA RIVER
SH 21 to US 59
46 Miles

Correct form, a properly balanced canoe, and life jackets are evidence that these canoeists are experienced at river running.

These children have learned the proper operation of a canoe and the safety precautions that will insure a lifetime of canoeing enjoyment.

to the US 59 crossing between Lufkin and Nacogdoches. Except during very dry periods, the inflow of some large creeks helps to make the stream flow adequate most of the time. (See map.) And since the river is now wider, it is easier to work a small boat or canoe around or through the frequent log jams. Again, be sure to get permission before using timber company lands along the way.

Access points along the way include a county road crossing between FM 1911 and FM 225 some 12 miles west of Nacogdoches. At the SH 7 crossing 12 miles southwest of Nacogdoches, there is a public boat ramp maintained by the Texas Parks and Wildlife Department (TPWD). From here it's 12 river miles to the US 59 crossing and another TPWD boat ramp. This area is typical hardwood bottomland, and during times of high water, the river can spread out over it with the channel sometimes losing its identity. Some young college students attempted to make a float through this sec-

Always pull your craft well up onto the shore or tie it securely to a solid fixture before leaving it for any length of time.

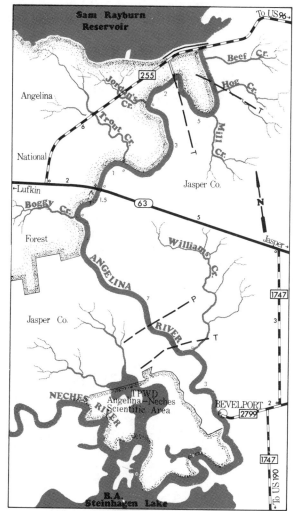

**ANGELINA RIVER
Sam Rayburn Reservoir to
Bevelport
17.5 Miles**

caps and rough water can form quickly on this open water as more than one fisherman has discovered.

The 17.5-mile section from the McGee Bend Dam to the junction of FM 2799 at Bevelport is said to be one of the most scenic stretches of river in East Texas. That it is, but at the time my wife and I made the trip in my bass boat one fall, the sand bars and even the drift logs had a coat of slime on them that made them extremely slick. For this reason we did not find a suitable place for an overnight camp along the way. An inquiry to the engineer at the dam brought this possible explanation: Most of the water released through the dam comes from near the bottom of the lake and therefore is loaded with silt and settlings from the decaying organic matter in the lake. Depending on the volume of water released, the river level is only raised a few feet before it falls again about as quickly as it came up. Since the current is rather slow even during the rise, the silt and other matter has a tendency to settle on the sand bars and other submerged objects along the way. During the more rainy season, this is not as much a problem.

There is a 5-mile section of the old river channel that "U-shapes" below the dam to the point where the spillway enters the river. This section can only be reached from this point, and at the time we were there, the shallows would have presented a problem for larger boats. The best place to begin on this section of the river is at SH 63 some 10 miles northwest of Jasper. There is a TPWD boat ramp and parking area here, and even though the river level was down below the end of the ramp, I had no trouble launching my bass boat on the packed sand. The river is sluggish with little or no current, and a canoeist will have no problem going either upstream or down.

The Angelina National Forest extends along the west bank for the upper portion of this section, and except for places where private camps are obvious, the shoreline is open. Be on the safe side, though, and ask before using.

It is another 11.5 miles from the SH 63 crossing to the TPWD boat ramp at Bevelport. There are a lot of private camps and summer homes along this stretch indicating its popularity over the years. From here to B. A. Steinhagen Lake, it is about 7 miles with an additional 4 miles across the open lake to the Martin Dies, Jr., State Park on the east shore near the US 190 crossing.

The "Little Angel" can offer a lot to the outdoor recreationist, but be sure to keep in mind that under the conditions of either high water or high winds on her lakes, she may not be so "angelic!"

tion during a flood a few years ago and got lost. They were found by searchers a couple of days later after they had been forced to spend two nights and a day marooned in a tree top. For this type of float, be sure to take a good compass and know how to use it. And don't forget to let some responsible person know where you are going and when you expect to return. Then, if you should get into trouble, help can get to you much sooner!

Just a few miles downstream the current virtually stops in the backwaters of Sam Rayburn Reservoir. The floater can go from US 59 all the way to the dam, but be careful on the big waters of the lake if you are using a canoe or small boat. White

Angelina River   **5**

Attoyac Bayou

Although listed among the major waterways of East Texas, Attoyac Bayou is impractical for floating even in a canoe or small flat-bottomed boat due to the many brush and log jams along its narrow length. From its beginning near the town of Mount Enterprise, it flows some 58 miles through farm and timberland to its junction with Sam Rayburn Reservoir on the Angelina River.

Local fishermen sing its praises because of the fine catfishing they enjoy, especially in the spring. Old-timers have told me about the sport of "grappling" where they simply waded the edges of the deeper holes, feeling with their hands up under the banks to "grapple" or grab big fish lying back in the dark waters! I know more than one who has a portion of finger missing as a result of finding something other than a catfish!

Some years ago I went fishing with a group of men from Garrison, Texas who were students in a Veterans Vocational Agriculture class. Our plan was to seine a section of the river using two-inch mesh chicken wire. With logging chains tied to the bottom to hold the wire down, half the group held the wire while the other half came down the river to sort of "drive" the fish into it.

Sure 'nuff, in one long shallow channel, we hemmed up "something" big enough to make a "V" wake as it tried to escape! It was worse than trying to catch a greased pig, but we finally managed to catch bare-handed a 14-pound buffalo fish. I doubt the legality of such fishing nowadays, so I wouldn't recommend it, but it was an experience I'll never forget!

There are several road crossings in Shelby, Nacogdoches, and San Augustine counties that offer access to the river. The private land owners will often give permission to cross their land to the river or bayou, and much of the shoreline is owned by large timber companies that frequently open their

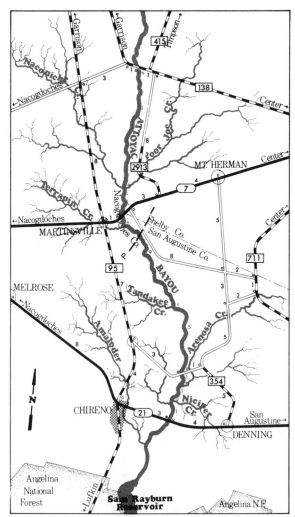

ATTOYAC BAYOU
FM 138 to SH 21
28 Miles

lands to the public for both hunting and fishing. However, a lot of these timberlands are currently being leased by hunting clubs and are closed to public use. Your best bet is to inquire locally for access information.

For those who wish to explore the Attoyac by boat or canoe, start from the point where it enters Sam Rayburn Reservoir below SH 103 east of Lufkin. This way, if you run into a brush or log jam, common to this stream, you will be able to return to your starting point. When there is an adequate flow of water, this can get you far enough up-river to enjoy plenty of seclusion. You just might find a hot-spot with plenty of those catfish and buffalo!

Big Cypress Bayou

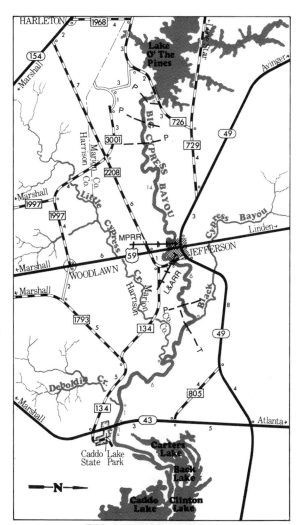

BIG CYPRESS BAYOU
Lake O' The Pines to
Caddo Lake State Park
34 Miles

Whatever this bayou lacks in the way of recreational opportunity by itself is more than made up for by the impoundments on it. The two older ones, Lake O' The Pines and Caddo Lake, as good as they are, are perhaps overshadowed by the "triplets" of hottest bass fishing, Lakes Montecello, Bob Sandlin, and Cypress Springs. These three on the headwaters have been stocked with the Florida strain of black bass, and the rapid growth they have shown has attracted fishermen from all over!

Sometimes referred to as Big Cypress Creek, this stream flows from the Bob Sandlin Dam just west of US 271 southeastward to Lake O' The Pines east of the US 259 crossing. Access is also available at the SH 11 crossing between these points making available two short floats through virgin hardwood forest with an abundance of wildlife. Keep in mind that varying water conditions sometimes make recreational use difficult. As on other streams of this width through timber country, there can be many log jams and downed trees to hinder the passage of any craft. The best chance for what could be a real exploration float is during a period of heavy run-off, but brush and log jams could still be a problem.

Camping and picnic facilities are maintained by the U.S. Army Corps of Engineers on Lake O' The Pines. Caddo Lake State Park is another fine spot for the river users.

Perhaps one of the more popular waterways in the state is that 34-mile section of the bayou between Lake O' The Pines and Caddo Lake State Park. Here one can readily understand whence comes the name of the bayou; it flows through almost jungle-like terrain crowded with big cypress trees. The use of the section downstream to Jefferson is mostly dependent on the release of water from the Ferrell's Bridge Dam that forms Lake O' The Pines. The normal release of only 5 cubic feet per second is not adequate, but during the spring,

fall, and winter periods, that can increase to as much as 1,000 CFS which results in very good water levels in the upper bayou.

In the early days of Texas, the city of Jefferson was a thriving center due to the shipping traffic that flowed up the bayou from Caddo Lake and on down to points south and east. Although the heyday has long passed, many tourists flock to the town during the historic pilgrimage held each May. And even today the bayou is wide and deep allowing even large motor boats to travel from Jefferson to Caddo Lake.

Access to this section begins at the crossing of US 59 one mile south of Jefferson. There is a boat ramp maintained by the Parks and Wildlife Department at the crossing of FM 134 in Jefferson. Another TPWD boat ramp is located at the SH 43 crossing only a mile above the park. Excellent facilities for camping are available in the park.

Blanco River

Flowing almost parallel to a portion of the Guadalupe River, the Blanco River travels through some of the most interesting scenery in the central part of Texas. It begins in the northeastern part of Kendall County and flows some 80 miles to the southeast through Blanco and Hays counties to unite with the San Marcos River just below the city of San Marcos. The area along the upper Blanco is noted for its historic Indian mounds and unusual geologic formations, while the lower section flows through baldcypress-lined banks. Except for periods of heavy rainfall, most of the river is shallow with only those areas behind low water dams having sufficient water for recreational use. And while there may be some interesting rapids and swift water during rainy times, keep this thought in mind before and during any float on the river: For the most part, the streambed *may* be privately owned. Find out for sure about the part you wish to float and get permission!

This is another one of those many times when I wish I were a lawyer or legislator or whatever it would take to make our trespass laws a bit less ambiguous. Being a landowner in the state of Texas, I am in sympathy with other landowners and our rights, but I am also concerned about the rights of the public to be able to use sensibly the waterways of Texas and the other states. It may just be wishful thinking, but I sure wish somebody could come up with a simple solution! Please forgive the digression; I just wanted to get in my two-cents worth!

The 23-mile section of the Blanco River above the town of Blanco is a narrow and extremely shallow stream that is not suitable except during periods of heavy run-off. Several small check dams are located in this area, particularly in the vicinity of Blanco. Blanco State Park has two of these. The Park, located on the river, makes a good access point for a trip downstream. It also has complete hookups and facilities for camping, picnicking, fishing and swimming.

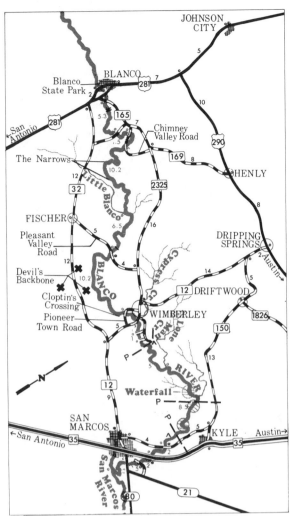

BLANCO RIVER
FM 165 to San Marcos River
64 Miles

While the map does show the river for a 64-mile run from Blanco to San Marcos, the river at normal levels does not have enough water flow until you get to the Devil's Backbone area west of Wimberley. Additional spring and creek inflows add to the recreational potential of the river below this point. During periods of heavy rainfall, this can be an excellent recreational waterway with numerous rapids and outstanding Hill Country scenery. The small check dams will have to be portaged, so be on the lookout for them.

From the FM 165 crossing just east of Blanco down to the last crossing above the Devil's Backbone area, there are three of these small dams and three county road crossings in the 25-mile section of the river. This last crossing above Devil's Backbone is the Pleasant Valley Road between FM 2325 and Fischer on FM 32. It should also be noted that the Little Blanco River adds a large volume of water to the flow of the Blanco above this crossing about 6 miles. Still another 6 miles down from the Pleasant Valley Road, the Devil's Backbone area with its hills rising several hundred feet above the river appears on the right.

Cloptin's Crossing is a ford located 2 miles southwest of Wimberley. This area was at one time being considered as the site for a major reservoir which would inundate several miles of the river, but no information is available as to the status of that plan. A short distance downstream is the Pio-

neer Town crossing, a county road one mile southwest of Wimberley. Cypress Creek, which has its origin in historic "Jacob's Well," enters a mile downstream and adds a large volume of water to the flow of the river.

FM 12 crosses just southeast of Wimberley with several county road crossings within the next few miles. A county park is located on the river west of Kyle. In addition to two other county road crossings, the river passes under IH 35 two miles northeast of San Marcos, and SH 80 crosses one mile east of San Marcos. About 3 miles below this crossing, the Blanco River flows into the San Marcos River, adding its volume to this popular waterway.

Your first stretch of whitewater is where you learn lessons in river "reading;" current flow, river direction, obstructions, and waves all tell a story.

Bosque River

Another of the somewhat smaller rivers of Central Texas, the Bosque River does offer some recreational opportunities in addition to those afforded by Lake Waco. The reservoir was built by the U.S. Army Corps of Engineers and supplies 7,270 acres of good fishing water and ample accommodations. Famous for its crappie fishing, the Texas Parks and Wildlife Department has also stocked other species in order to broaden the recreational base.

The Bosque rises in northern Erath County and travels about 115 miles through Hamilton, Bosque, and McLennan counties to its junction with the Brazos River at Waco. While it is a perennially flowing stream, its use as a recreational waterway is restricted to periods of heavy rainfall. About the only hazards are the low-hanging limbs or trees.

The 35-mile section of the Bosque between Iredell and Clifton has the potential of an excellent waterway with few hazards when rainfall is plentiful. During these times, there will be a few fast stretches to lend excitement to a float. During periods of normal flow, the river is not very wide and there are many stretches that are too shallow for good recreational use.

The best point for putting in is at the SH 6 crossing 2 miles west of Iredell although the access here is poor. The crossing of FM 216 in Iredell 2 miles downstream also offers poor access to the river. About 2 miles east of Iredell is a county road crossing off FM 927 where about 700 feet of shoreline and a small parking area are available. Another county road crosses between SH 6 and SH 144 some 6 miles downriver. The SH 22 crossing in the town of Meridian offers 200 feet of shoreline and a small parking area. When the water flow is high enough, this 14-mile portion of the Bosque makes a fine day float from Meridian down to FM 219 on the eastern edge of Clifton. There is about 200 feet of shoreline and picnic tables available here.

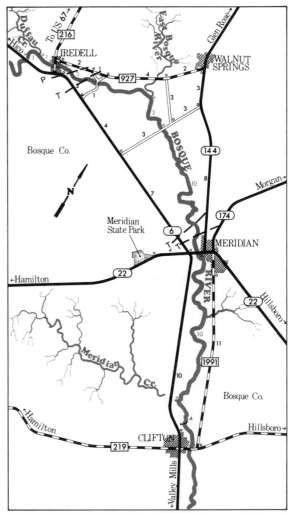

BOSQUE RIVER
Iredell to Clifton
35 Miles

The 34-mile section of the Bosque from Clifton to Waco and its junction with the Brazos River usually has enough water for recreational use at all times. Lake Waco is located on this section, and the water above the impoundment deepens considerably. Below the dam, the flow depends on the release of water from the dam. Usually, there is adequate water here partly because of the existence of Lake Brazos which is located just below the point where the Bosque joins the Brazos. This is a short but very scenic area as the Bosque winds below the massive limestone bluffs called Lover's Leap in Cameron Park. For a more extended trip, consult the section detailing the Brazos River.

Brazos River

I think it was Mark Twain who once made reference to the "soul" of a river in some of his writings about the Mississippi. If it is a characteristic attributed to any stream, surely the Brazos, so closely linked with legend and Texas history, can qualify! The largest river between the Rio Grande and the Red, it is approximately 840 miles from the source of its longest fork to the Gulf of Mexico.

The original name of the river was Brazos de Dios meaning "Arms of God." There are several interesting legends as to why it was given this name. One is that the Coronado expedition, wandering on the trackless Llano Estacado, exhausted its water and was threatened with death from thirst. Arriving at the bank of the river they gave it the name of Brazos de Dios in thankfulness. Another story tells that a ship in the Gulf exhausted its fresh water supply, and its crew was saved when they found the mouth of the Brazos.

Still another story is that miners on the San Saba were forced by drouth to seek water near present day Waco, and they called it Brazos de Dios in thankfulness. There is also the theory that the early Spanish map-makers called it "Arms of God" because of the great spread of its tributaries.

Many of the early Anglo-American settlements in Texas were located within the Brazos valley. San Felipe de Austin, the capital of Austin's colony, and Washington-on-the Brazos where Texans declared their independence, are two examples. There was some navigation of the lower section of the river during this time. Today, the river intersects the Intracoastal Waterway near Freeport.

An annual commemoration ceremony is held at the Washington-on-the Brazos State Historical Park on the Sunday nearest the date of March 2, for it was on this date in 1836 that Texas declared its independence from Mexico.

Most of the Brazos Valley is under the control of the Brazos River Authority which conducts a multipurpose program of development. There are

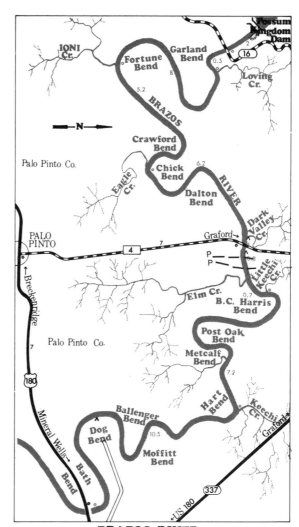

**BRAZOS RIVER
POSSUM KINGDOM DAM TO US 180
41.4 Miles**

three large reservoirs on the Brazos, Possum Kingdom, Granbury, and Whitney. These reservoirs offer some major fishing opportunities. The first successful natural spawn of striped bass in Texas has been recorded on the river between Lakes Whitney and Granbury. The tailrace below the Possum Kingdom Dam is perhaps the leading spot in the state for put-and-take rainbow trout fishing. There is about one mile of shoreline near the State Highway Department bridge, and some 3 miles of wade fishing is open to the public. For more information on this site, call the Possum Kingdom State Fish Hatchery at 817/779-2301. The entire Brazos River system including the three big lakes is also an excellent white bass fishery.

Of the three upper forks of the Brazos, only the Clear Fork has much potential for recreational use on a year-round basis. The Double Mountain Fork and the Salt Fork come together in Stonewall County to form the main river; there still is insufficient water for recreational use until the Clear Fork joins in Young County. For those who may try to float the Clear Fork during periods of heavy run-off, there are two danger points. One is a small 3-foot waterfall about one mile up-stream from the US 180 crossing. Then, between US 180 and US 380, a dam backs up a lake for about 4 miles. Just below this dam, there is a series of dangerous stair-stepped falls where the water flows over two rock ledges approximately 20 feet high. Naturally, a portage is required.

Even though it is some 150 miles from the point where the three forks come together to the backed-up waters of Possum Kingdom Reservoir, only that 25-mile stretch from where the Clear Fork joins the river has enough water for recreational use.

The 41.4-mile section immediately below Possum Kingdom Reservoir is probably one of the most popular as well as the most scenic stretches of the Brazos River. And although the flow of the river depends on the amount of water being released through the dam, a trip downstream by canoe is possible though difficult. When electricity is being generated at the dam, it is common for the river level to rise as much as two or three feet in a matter of minutes. Campers using the sand bars and islands for both day use and overnight should keep this in mind when selecting a campsite. There are even a couple of good rapids during high water, one of them being beneath the FM 4 bridge.

Information compiled by Texas Parks and Wildlife Department biologists provides an interesting side-light to this section of the Brazos. The biologists made a profile of the river and assessed the fish populations, flow rates, tributary inflows, gradients, and water quality. The Brazos in this area is unique because of the extreme fluctuations in flow rates caused by water releases. According to the biologists, when the river is down for awhile, the water warms up. Then large releases of extremely cold water change the water temperature very quickly.

One of the purposes of this study is to learn if smallmouth bass, already making good progress after being stocked in a number of Texas rivers and lakes, can adapt well enough in the chilly Brazos to establish a fishery. Rainbow trout are stocked usually at two-week intervals during the winter months along this section.

Although no facilities are provided, the Brazos River Authority land immediately below the dam is open to the public. You may prefer to launch 2 miles downstream at the SH 16 crossing where

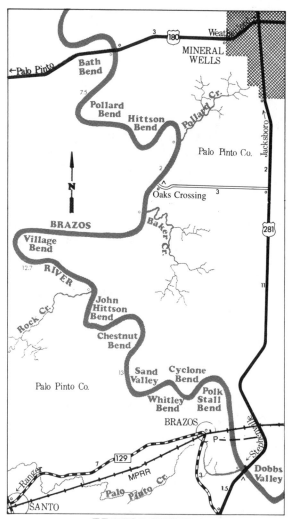

BRAZOS RIVER
US 180 to US 281
35.2 Miles

good access is offered in a small area below the crossing. It is then 20 miles of scenic river that flows through outcroppings of rock, high bluffs, and occasional views of the Palo Pinto Mountains. There is a private camp on the north bank of the river just before you reach the FM 4 crossing. Don't forget about the rapids beneath the bridge. There is no access to the river here except by private road where you may be charged a fee. This 20-mile stretch makes a good two-day float with time to enjoy the river.

The next access point is just over 15 miles downstream from the FM 4 crossing at a private camp west of Mineral Wells on a county road off US 180. Tables are provided and overnight camping is permitted. Natural campsites on the sand and gravel bars are fairly plentiful also. Another 4 miles gets you to the US 180 crossing where there is only limited access to the river.

The next 35-mile section between US 180 and US 281 is very similar to this last one in that it continues on through the cedar-covered hills and steep, brush-covered banks. The time to catch the best water level for floating is a day or two after water has been released for generation of power at the dam. This gives the water time to get below US 180. If no water is being released, there will be many shallow areas. The Corps of Engineers at the dam will give you information on when water is being released.

For a short float or an alternate launching site, there is Oaks Crossing 8.5 miles below US 180 with a private campground. Another 25 miles will get you to the Pleasant Valley Canoe Rental and Shuttle Service where limited camping is available for a fee. It is about 24 miles from here to the US 281 crossing; that's a long float so be prepared. Try to schedule plenty of time for enjoying the scenery, the solitude, and the fishing. If you enjoy primitive camping, the many small islands to be found in this stretch as well as numerous sand bars offer plenty of places to camp. Just be sure to stay above the high-water level.

There is reportedly a private camp at the US 281 crossing where picnicking and camping facilities are available. Good river access is offered at this point.

As you move into the 41-mile section from US 281 down to the crossing of FM 1884, the surrounding terrain changes to more open country and the river becomes a slow meandering stream with many bends and twists. It is very wide, and in places shallow, but there is usually enough water for recreational use. The next access point is at the IH 20 crossing some 14 miles southwest of Weatherford and about 12.2 miles downstream. There are three private camps in this area that offer access but their facilities are limited. J. W.'s Canoe and Kayak Rental located here offers shuttle service, too.

There is another private camp at the FM 1543 crossing 15 miles downstream near Dennis with access but limited facilities. The next crossing and campsite access is at FM 1884, some 13.7 miles downstream. The river enters the upper portion of Lake Granbury in about 4 miles.

Lake Granbury, also known as the De Cordova Bend Dam and Reservoir, is the second of the three large lakes on the Brazos. In the past, the tailrace area below the dam has been closed to fishing during March and April to protect striped bass which congregate below the dam for their spring

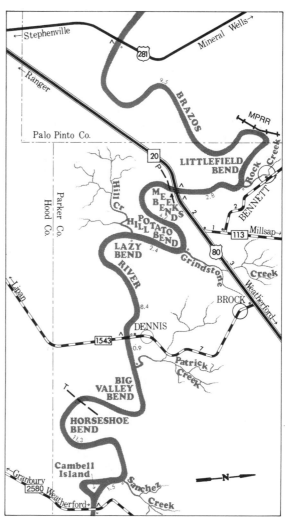

BRAZOS RIVER
US 281 to FM 1884
41 Miles

Fishing the rapids can be as enjoyable for the ardent fisherman as running them is for the canoeist.

spawning run. The closed area extends from the dam about 0.2 mile downstream to the Brazos River Authority property line.

The water level of the 39-mile section between Lake Granbury and the Lake Whitney Recreation Area depends on the release of water through the De Cordova Bend Dam. When it is not generating, the water level is low until you reach the backwaters of Lake Whitney. It is about 30 miles to the first crossing at US 67 and another 3 miles to the FM 200 crossing. There is access at the US 67 crossing on the east bank; the trail is difficult, but there is a road extending from the highway to the top of the high bank below the bridge. There are some private camps and canoe rental agencies in this area that also offer shuttle service. Unless you can allow plenty of time for floating this upper portion

of the Brazos, you'll likely miss a lot of the fun that it has to offer.

Another 6 miles will get you to the Lake Whitney Recreational Area where camping and picnicking facilities are available. This area extends about 36 miles up the river from Lake Whitney making a total of approximately 75 miles of recreational waterway from the Lake Granbury Dam to Lake Whitney. Two additional access points are a county road crossing off FM 200 some 15 miles southwest of Cleburne and the SH 174 crossing some 6 miles west of Blum.

Another 39-mile section lies between the Lake Whitney Dam and the US 84 crossing on Waco Drive Bridge in Waco. There are many good springs in this area that add to the excellent quality of the very cold water that comes through the dam

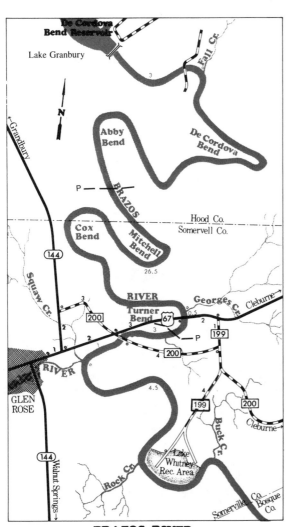

BRAZOS RIVER
De Cordova Bend Dam To
Whitney Recreation Area
39 Miles

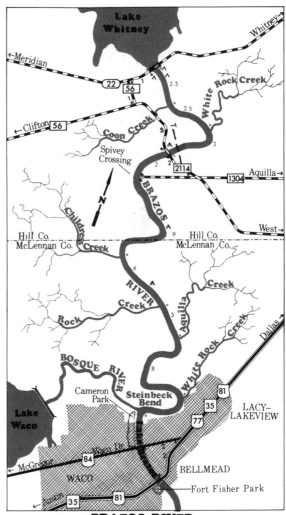

BRAZOS RIVER
Whitney Dam to Waco Drive Bridge
39 Miles

from the bottom of the lake. However, unless the power station is generating, there will be shallow areas. There are a few small rapids, but none of these are considered hazardous. There are several private camps in addition to the Corps of Engineers parks and a state park on Whitney as well as natural campsites that provide more than adequate camping locations. Three private camps are located off SH 22 just below the dam. Another is located near the FM 2114 crossing 5 miles south of the dam. There is also a private camp off FM 1304 at a spot known as Spivey Crossing.

The Bosque River enters on the right a short distance from the Waco city limits. The river gets deeper here and through the city and is known as Lake Brazos. There are several access points along the river beginning with the Lake Shore-FM 3051 crossing and continuing all the way to Fort Fisher Park past the IH 35 crossing. The Homer Garrison Memorial Museum, once the headquarters of the Texas Rangers, is located in the restored Fort Fisher and is the focal point of the park.

The next crossing is about one mile down from SH 6-US 77-US 81. The dam forming the Brazos River Lake within the city of Waco is 0.5 mile below this crossing and a portage around is required. Water releases at this dam are automatic; when the lake rises above the top of the conservation pool, the spillway opens to release water.

There are no more road crossings until the river reaches SH 7 some 5 miles west of Marlin. A TPWD boat ramp is provided here. The water of the Brazos is beginning to lose the clarity that it had after coming through the large impoundments. It is oftentimes quite muddy-looking from here on due to the run-off from the sandy banks and the watershed. Most of the river bottom lands throughout this area are in cultivation.

From SH 7 to FM 979 west of Calvert is a 28-mile stretch that has one potentially hazardous point about 3 miles downstream from the SH 7 crossing. This is known as Falls-on-the-Brazos, a small waterfall that reaches all the way across the river. There is also a concrete low water crossing and a TPWD boat ramp. The falls are navigable if the water level is fairly high. Always take the time to stop and walk ahead to inspect any stretch of water of which you are unsure. FM 413 crosses some 11 miles downstream and it is another 14 miles to the FM 979 crossing.

With one exception, the 315 miles on to the Gulf near Freeport offer little variation to the floater traveling through the farm and ranch land where early Texas history was made. The water level is usually high enough for recreational use year round. Strong southerly winds can be a problem for the boater due to the very wide channel.

The exception I mentioned is a section of river that Ben Nolen and Bob Narramore in their book, *Texas Rivers and Rapids*, said should not be called a "float trip," but a "run the rapids, turn around and run 'em again" type of river! Known as Hidalgo

A group outing always makes a river adventure more fun. Experienced canoeists should be placed at the front, middle, and rear of the group.

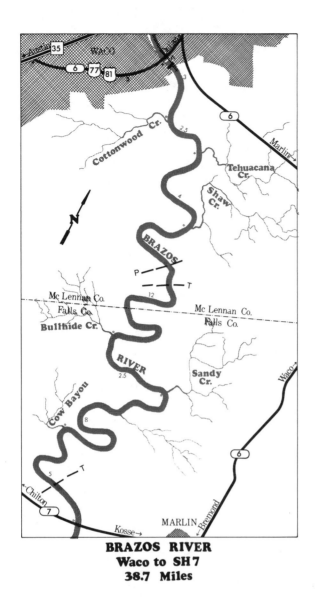

BRAZOS RIVER
Waco to SH 7
38.7 Miles

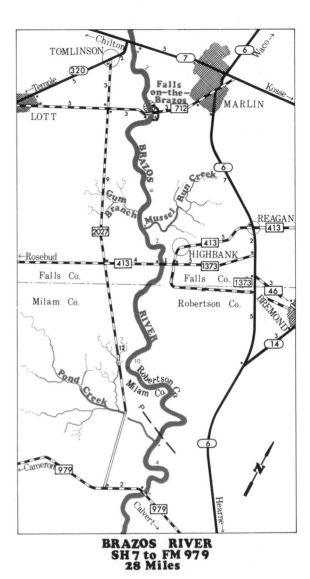

BRAZOS RIVER
SH 7 to FM 979
28 Miles

Falls, the rapid here is about one-fourth mile long and can reach Class IV levels when the river is high. This can mean high standing waves and spots that require precise maneuvering, and as they say, the time to make it is anytime you don't mind getting wet!

The Brazos River Resort located at the SH 105 crossing west of Navasota is the best put-in and take-out point for getting to Hidalgo Falls. The shallow water along the left bank allows both the canoeist and the kayak floaters to get above the falls after each run of the rapids. Good camping areas are available at the resort, but the facilities are limited. There is a small fee for launching and use of the camp. For timely information on the river flow, call the resort at either 409/825-2775 or 409/

825-7378. The Falls are located approximately 4 miles upstream from SH 105.

If after a float you have failed to discover the aforementioned "soul" of the Brazos and the tremendous effect that it has had on the history and the life of Texans, then perhaps you need to follow its course again. Then again, you may be one who sees a river only as a stretch of water for floating, fishing, and camping. I greatly enjoy all those things, too, but for me, the pleasure and the thrills are much greater when I can sit around a late-evening campfire on a clean sandbar and think of those who preceded me down through the years. And sometimes I wonder who will follow me and what they will find along this great river a hundred years from now?

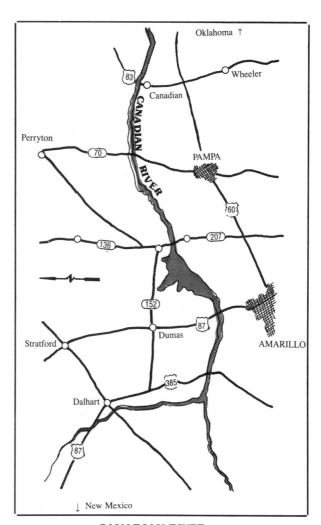

CANADIAN RIVER

Canadian River

Although the Canadian River is not usually listed as one of the major rivers of Texas, I feel that it should be mentioned if only because of the importance given to it by the early cattle drivers on their way north. They classed it as one of the important milestones they reached on their long journey.

Your state highway map will show that it crosses the Texas Panhandle just north of Amarillo to enter Oklahoma north of SH 33. As for the recreational opportunities, the river itself has little to offer since the flow cannot be depended on. But wait! There in the center of the Panhandle on the Canadian River is Lake Meredith, a 21,000-acre reservoir built by the U.S. Bureau of Reclamation, that is perhaps the outstanding spot for water-oriented recreation in that portion of the state. It has also produced the state record walleye. Consult *A Guide to Fishing in Texas* (Lone Star Books, Houston, Texas) for more information on this great lake on the Canadian River.

It doesn't take much water to provide fishin' fun for the bank fisherman.

Colorado River

For me, there is magic in the word "Colorado," especially when it is applied to the river. Whether or not this stems from stories and legends connected with another river by the same name up in the states of Colorado, Utah, and Arizona, I do not know. I do know that both of these mighty rivers are entitled to love and respect from anyone who enjoys the vast recreational opportunities they offer. A raft trip through the mighty canyons of that western river can possibly be the highlight of a lifetime of adventure. Fishing in some of the great reservoirs that have been built along its course can be tremendous. But the Texas Colorado River can also offer a lot of challenge to both the fisherman and the outdoorsman who likes to use a river to get away from it all!

From its beginning way out in Dawson County in West Texas, the Colorado River flows some 600 miles to the southeast to enter Matagorda Bay on the Gulf. Measured by length and drainage area, it is the largest river wholly in Texas. (The Brazos is excluded from this comparison since its drainage basin extends into New Mexico.) Its name is a Spanish word meaning "reddish." It is thought that the name was given by the early Spanish explorers to the muddy Brazos and that Spanish mapmakers later transposed the two names.

The upper reaches of the river flow through usually prairie terrain until the river reaches San Saba County where it enters the rugged Hill Country and Burnet-Llano Basin.

The principal area for recreational use within the upper portion of the river lies on or just above the two reservoirs that have been formed by dams on this section. The first of these is Lake J. B. Thomas southwest of Snyder in Borden and Scurry Counties. The other is E. V. Spence Reservoir in Coke County north of San Angelo. The still waters above these reservoirs are suitable for recreational use as are short portions below the dams when water is being released.

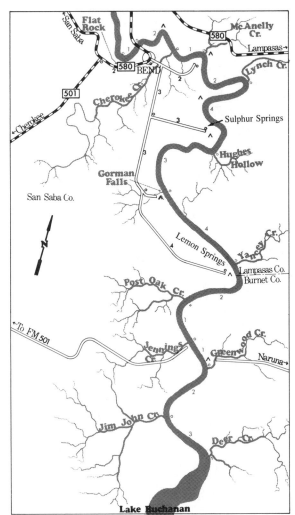

COLORADO RIVER
Flat Rock to Lake Buchanan
26 Miles

After reaching the Hill Country and Burnet-Llano Basin, the river flows through a picturesque series of canyons until it issues from the Balcones Escarpment at Austin to continue on through the Coastal Plain to the Gulf. A series of reservoirs has been constructed through this area that is known as the Highland Chain of Lakes. The two largest are Lake Buchanan and Lake Travis. Between these two are three smaller ones: Inks, L. B. J. (formerly Granite Shoals), and Marble Falls. Below Lake Travis is Lake Austin, an older lake that is largely filled with silt. Town Lake is located within the city of Austin.

Anglo-Americans settled on the banks of the lower Colorado as early as the 1820s, and in 1839 the Capital Commission of the Republic of Texas chose the area where the river flows from the Balcones Escarpment as the site of the new capital of the Republic. When Texas became a state, Austin remained the capital. There was some navigation along the lower channel and boats occasionally ventured as far upstream as Austin, but a natural log "raft" formed in the channel near the Gulf, blocking river traffic.

The conservation and utilization of the waters of the Colorado are under the jurisdiction of three agencies created by the state Legislature, the Lower, Central, and Upper Colorado River Authorities. An interesting side-light is that one of its tributaries, Pecan Bayou which joins the main stream southwest of Goldthwaite in Mills County, is the farthest west bayou in the United States.

Generally, use of the Colorado for recreational purposes best begins in the 26-mile section above Lake Buchanan in San Saba, Llano, Lampasas, and Burnet Counties. It is a very scenic area with high limestone bluffs, vistas of rugged, cedar-covered hills, and one of the most spectacular waterfalls in Texas, Gorman Falls. It is formed where the waters of Gorman Creek tumble into the Colorado over a 75-foot limestone bluff! The river itself is rather wide and relatively shallow in this area. During the dry months especially, due to the use of river water for irrigation upstream, floating the Colorado this far above Lake Buchanan can be a problem.

This is an area that is famous for its fishing for white or sand bass during the spawning run that normally gets under way a couple of weeks before the Easter holidays. Here again the flow of the river and the level of the lake below can make a difference in the fishing. Near the little community of Bend, the state acquired in 1984 a 712-acre site at Gorman Falls as a future park site. The area had been operated as a fishing camp until its closing some two years before. In May of 1988, the state formally opened Colorado Bend State Park at the former site of the Lemon's Fishing Camp some four miles downstream. The Park opened with primitive camping, backpacking and river fishing. The park entrance is about four miles from Bend via an unpaved road. Fishing is best done in a shallow draft canoe or johnboat, and some prefer to do it from a float tube of some sort.

Speaking of white bass on the Colorado, the world record of this species came from the river just below Longhorn Dam in late March of 1977. It weighed 5 pounds 9 ounces and was 20¾ inches long with a girth of 17 inches!

A Texas state record fish was also caught in Lake Buchanan in February of 1982. This was a Guadalupe spotted bass weighing 2 pounds, 4 ounces that established a new category in the state record books. Found mainly in the Upper Colorado and

Guadalupe River systems as well as some of the smaller drainages in the Edwards Plateau region, Guadalupe spotted bass normally are smaller than their cousins, the Kentucky spotted bass.

While the impoundments and the river itself offer fine fishing for other bass and catfish, the striped bass has really done well with the state record, caught in Lake Austin by Harry Lamb of Austin in 1981, tipping the scales at 38¼ pounds! A 43¾-pounder reportedly caught below Longhorn Dam was never certified. To further convince you of the fishing potential of this great river system, the state record smallmouth bass weighing 5 pounds, 12 ounces was caught here, too, in March of 1980!

Extensive studies of the fisheries of the river have been made by TPWD biologists as they work for more complete and better utilization of this resource.

But going back to that section immediately above Lake Buchanan and following the map as we move downstream, let's examine the features and the recreational potential.

Flat Rock, so called because of a large limestone slab that extends from Ranch Road 580 to the river, is located about a mile west of the community of Bend. This is the best spot to "put in" for the float; the access is poor at the crossing of RR 580 about one mile downstream. Other access points along this portion of the river include the Sulphur Springs Camp 8 miles down from Flat Rock, the new Colorado Bend State Park, formerly known as Gorman Falls and Lemon Springs Camps. There is a charge for camping and entry and the use of the facilities, but they are the best along the way.

One should keep in mind that this is deer hunting country, and the camp roads and camp areas are closed during the open season.

There are enough shallow rapids along this stretch to make the trip exciting, the first one is just above the bridge crossing at Bend. There are others between there and just below the intersection of Cherokee Creek a couple of miles downstream. A great spot for the photographer is Barefoot Falls below where Lynch Creek joins the river.

The backwaters of Lake Buchanan are evident at about 10 or 11 miles below Colorado Bend State Park. A county road off FM 501 and another out of Naruna in Burnet County are the only other access points in this area. Some shoreline is available, but at the latest report, no facilities. Of course there are numerous access points around the lake and excellent facilities for the outdoor recreationist.

We will leave the portion of the Colorado that is known as the Highland Chain of Lakes to the lake

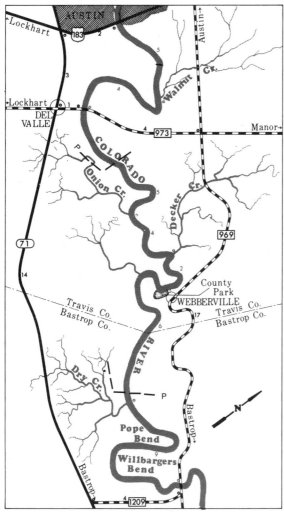

COLORADO RIVER
US 183 To FM 969
36 Miles

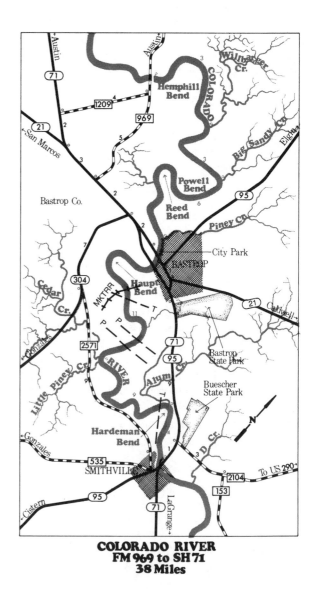

COLORADO RIVER
FM 969 to SH 71
38 Miles

enthusiasts and drop down to just below the city of Austin to the US 183 crossing known as the Montopolis Bridge in East Austin. A road leads down to a gently sloping bank with very good access to the river. Be on the lookout for a small dam some 3 miles downriver where a portage is required. The next crossing is at FM 973 about one mile northeast of Del Valle another 6 miles downstream. The next access is at the county park in the community of Webberville another 11 miles down. Campsites with picnic tables are available along with a launching ramp and good access to the river. This point is only about 10 miles from Austin by way of FM 969 and can be either a good put-in or take-out point. The next crossing is that of FM 969 some 5 miles northwest of Bastrop. A TPWD boat ramp gives good access here at a point on the river about 16 miles below the Webberville county park.

The next 38-mile section of the river lies within Bastrop County. As in the above portion, the amount of flow is determined by the amount of water coming through the Highland Chain. Since there is a fairly continuous release through Longhorn Dam at Town Lake, there is normally enough for recreational use. Campers on sand bars should take care to locate above the highwater mark or they can wake up with a very wet camp. A friend of mine had to learn this the hard, or should I say "wet," way!

The next access is at the City Park in Bastrop 13 miles downstream from the FM 969 crossing. The park is reached by following Main Street to Farm Street which will lead to the river. There is a boat ramp here and picnic tables are available. The next two bridge crossings in south Bastrop, SH 21 and SH 71–95, do not offer any means of access to the river. However, if one should need a campsite in

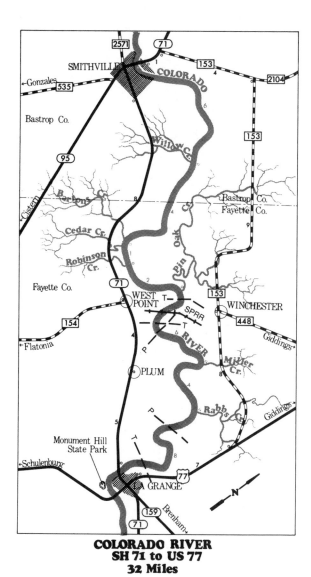

COLORADO RIVER
SH 71 to US 77
32 Miles

only a very few places with swift water and minor rapids. The river is best described as a slow, meandering stream with several large cliffs and cutbanks. It is reported that petrified logs and fossils have been discovered in some of these. There are sand bars along the way for day use or camping.

Several large creeks join the main channel along this section, but the next access crossing is that of SH 71 on the southwest edge of La Grange. There is a boat ramp here with good access and a small camping area. It is only a mile on down to the crossing of US 77, but the access here is poor. However, Monument Hill State Park is located on the right about half way between these crossings with only picnic facilities available. The 4-acre park has a memorial shaft dedicated to Captain Nicholas Dawson and his men who fought at Salado Creek in the war for Texas' independence from Mexico and to the men of the "black bean lottery" of the Mier Expedition of 1842. The bodies of these heroes were brought to Monument Hill for reburial in 1848.

From this point on to the Gulf and Matagorda Bay is about 186 miles of slow-moving yet scenic coastal river. The first 43 miles from La Grange to Columbus can be a pleasant float except during extremely dry, hot seasons. There are several large islands as well as numerous sand bars that offer campsites for day and overnight use. And although it does improve the quantity of the flow, any appreciable amount of rain can cause this section of the river to become muddy although it is still virtually unpolluted.

The first crossing below US 77 is just north of Columbus on SH 71 at the 35-mile point. There is a boat ramp here along with public camping areas in the Columbus Chamber of Commerce Park. The river then makes a 6.5-mile loop to the east before returning to the US 90 crossing east of town. There is river access here, but it is rather long and difficult. This short loop can make a pleasant trip for a day's outing.

For information on the various sections between the road crossings from here on to the Gulf, I suggest that you consult the county highway maps that are available, incidentally, for every county in Texas. About the only problem you are likely to encounter is a strong southeasterly wind that can make progress along the wide channel more difficult.

Regardless of where you go on the Colorado River, you have seen some of the best that Texas has to offer, and very likely you have trod in the footsteps of some of our famous ancestors!

this area, the Bastrop State Park has a large, beautiful campground with all facilities located just east of town in the forks of SH 21 and SH 71–95. The famous "Lost Pines" of Texas are the setting for this park. Some of the scenery along the next section of the Colorado will remind you of the piney woods of East Texas.

The Lower Colorado River Authority some years ago initiated a project to improve the access points and suitable camping areas along the portion between Bastrop and Smithville. There are several islands and sand bars suitable for camping and day use in this 25-mile stretch from the Bastrop City Park to the SH 71 crossing in Smithville. A TPWD boat ramp is available here.

From this point in Smithville, it is 32 miles down to the crossing of US 77 south of La Grange with

Concho River

The main stream of the Concho River is formed when its three forks, the North, Middle, and South, come together in the city of San Angelo. While the North and Middle forks are relatively long, there is not enough flow for recreational use until slack water above the reservoirs is reached. There are three major lakes on the forks of the Concho above their junction. Lake O. C. Fisher was built on the North Fork by the U.S. Corps of Engineers in 1947. Twin Buttes Reservoir and Lake Nasworthy just south of San Angelo on the South and Middle Forks combine to make for outstanding fishing (See *A Guide to Fishing in Texas*, Lone Star Books, Houston, Texas, for more information on these three great fishin' holes!) Naturally, the flow of the river is dependent on water releases from these reservoirs.

The Concho itself is not a long river by the usual Texas standards, but it is a scenic one as it flows through 24 miles of Tom Green County and another 29 miles through Concho County to its junction with the Colorado River.

From the dam of O. C. Fisher Lake on the North Fork down to the Bell Street City Park in San Angelo is an 8-mile stretch which is suitable for recreational use when the dam is releasing water. It is here that the forks come together to form the main stream. Also, when Lake Nasworthy is releasing water, there is a short stretch of the South Fork that is usable above the junction at the Bell Street City Park.

Although it is not mapped here, there is an 18-mile section of the main stream from South Concho Park in San Angelo to the FM 1692 crossing that has a minimum amount of water for recreational use most of the time. There are two low water dams along the way that can pose problems in the use of the river. Access to this portion of the river is no problem because of the existence of several parks including the South Concho City Park in San Angelo and two county parks at downstream low-water crossings.

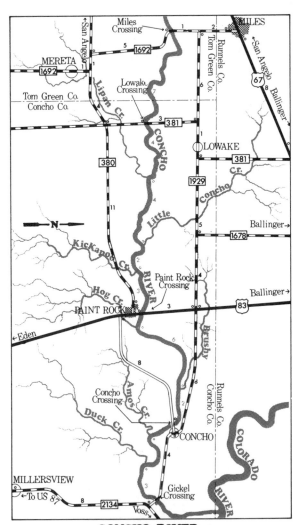

CONCHO RIVER
FM 1692 to Gickel Crossing
35 Miles

The quiet that accompanies canoeing enables paddlers to view a good sampling of wildlife.

The next section of the Concho is a 35-mile stretch from FM 1692 to a county road off FM 2134 some 11 miles east of Paint Rock. Except for extended periods of dry weather, there is normally sufficient water for recreational use. There are a few small rapids and swift areas, but none that will give you serious problems. The major problems along this stretch are the several small dams and low-water crossings with rather deep, still water above that require a portage.

At the FM 1692 crossing, known as Miles Crossing, some 12 miles northeast of San Angelo, there is a small county park located on the south bank with good access. The next road crossing is that of FM 381 some 7 miles downstream, but access here

Even one person can successfully portage a rough stretch of water as illustrated here. This precaution sometimes saves money, equipment, and lives.

Part of the adventure of canoeing is reaching places inaccessible by automobile.

is fenced off. US 83 crosses the river 13 miles farther down in the Paint Rock community. Highway access is poor, but there is a low-water crossing approximately 100 yards downstream that does offer good access. There used to be an old city park and swimming pool here, but no more. There is a low-water dam between the highway and the low-water crossing.

A county road crossing off FM 1929, known as the Concho Crossing, lies about 7 miles northeast of Paint Rock. There is good access here and the river is wide and deep above this crossing, changing to shallow and narrow below. The Gickel Crossing off FM 2134 some 7 miles downstream is 11 miles east of Paint Rock and also offers good access. It isn't far from this point on to the junction of the Concho with the Colorado River.

Devil's River

My first introduction to the Devil's River was from high above on one of the bluffs overlooking a few scattered pools of greenish-looking water. Actually, I was hunting for whitetail deer in this country of broken canyons, rock, and cactus-covered plateaus. In a land where it is said that everything will either stick you or bite you, the river seemed very out of place.

The actual point of origin of the Devil's River is hard to determine since the upper portions are dry except during and shortly after heavy rains. The county maps of Crockett, Schleicher, Sutton, and Val Verde all show sections of it; parts of these are simply named Dry Devil's River Draw. A few years back my wife and I were traveling on FM 189 in the southwest corner of Sutton County on the way to Juno. This road crosses the usually dry bed of the river right at the Val Verde County line. It crosses it four more times before it reaches SH 163 just north of Juno. This happened to be one of those times when heavy rains the night before up north were sending flash floods downriver. It caught us just right to make us wait at each crossing. At one of these where the water was more than a hundred yards wide, we drove through in the camper behind a couple of men who walked ahead of us to show the depth and to make sure there were no washouts.

I'm not sure but I think the roughness of the terrain through which it flows and the might of those sudden floods is why they call it the Devil's River! It sure is rugged country, but the folks who live there love it. I'll have to admit that it's a nice place to visit, but I wouldn't want to live there!

Any use of the river for recreational purposes is seasonal at best except for the far downstream section near where it joins the Rio Grande near Del Rio. With a total length of nearly 100 miles, in some stretches it goes completely underground to rise again downstream, fed by springs and the few spring-fed creeks that have a somewhat regular

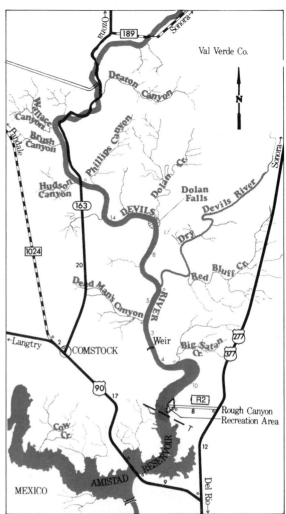

DEVILS RIVER
SH 163 to
Rough Canyon Recreation Area
44 Miles

flow. Except for the periods of flooding, the water is of exceptional quality as it flows over and through sand and gravel deposits.

Before taking a look at the lower portion of the Devil's River that does offer recreational opportunity, let me mention that the rough country of Val Verde County and the surrounding area was once a popular area for early Indian tribes. During a deer hunt, I photographed several Indian drawings on the walls of the large sheltered ledges within the canyons. It would indeed be a ''hot spot'' for anyone interested in the history and life styles of these early inhabitants. At the time I was there, the land was privately owned, and I'm sure it still is. Get permission!

Beginning at the southernmost crossing of SH 163 there is a 44-mile section down to the Rough

Canyon Recreation Area on Lake Amistad. The water flow at first is low, but it picks up gradually as more springs and spring-fed creeks join the river. The river flows through a narrow valley that becomes almost canyon-like at times. In many places, the river bed appears to be of solid rock carved out by many centuries of action from moving currents. There are several rapids that may have to be portaged depending on the height of the water, and there is one major falls, Dolan Falls, where the drop is reportedly about 25 feet.

There are certain areas along the course of the river that, during the times of high flood, the waters rush through with the "roar of the devil!" This is perhaps another version of how the river got its name. No matter which part of the river you happen to be on, be alert for those sudden flash floods. Just as in all arid and mountainous terrain, it doesn't have to rain where you are to put you in danger of flooding. A heavy downfall as much as a hundred miles away can send a wall of water rushing down on you, especially if you are in a narrow valley or canyon.

Dolan Falls is located about 14 miles below the SH 163 crossing known as Baker's Crossing. This crossing is 20 miles north of the town of Comstock where SH 163 joins US 90. The Falls are located just below the point where Dolan Creek flows in from the left. They are magnificent, reaching all the way across the river, and are one of the largest falls in all the state. Of course, a portage is necessary.

Now the river begins to widen out and gradually get deeper with an abundance of rapids. Depending on the height of the flow, be careful in running any rapids of consequence without first taking a look-see. Better to be safe than sorry.

Some 8 miles below the falls another stream enters the main channel, and this one really is named Dry Devil's River! On the right another 5 miles downriver is Dead Man's Canyon, possibly so named for the demise of some early traveler. Approximately 3 miles farther is an International Boundary Commission weir dam. Below this point, the Devil's River widens out and takes on the appearance of an arm of Amistad Reservoir on the Rio Grande. It is 14 miles on to the Rough Canyon Recreation Area 12 miles northwest of Del Rio. It is 8 miles west of US 277/377 and is administered by the National Park Service with access and primitive camping available. Be careful of high winds on the open water. It can get pretty rough.

The beauty and majesty of the canyons of West Texas waterways are well worth the travel required to reach them.

Frio River

The Frio River has its beginning in the northeastern part of Real County and flows southeast through Uvalde, Medina, Frio, La Salle, and Live Oak counties for about 250 miles to the vicinity of Three Rivers where it joins the Nueces and Atascosa Rivers. The upper section is spring fed as it flows through picturesque canyons. It is a free-flowing river with no major impoundments.

The 31-mile section from the point where Kent Creek joins the Frio some 9 miles north of Leakey downstream to near Concan is the most suited for recreational use. The springs in this upper section give the narrow stream a flow of about 100 cubic feet per second at normal levels. The flow may be a bit intermittent on the 10 miles above Leakey.

The first access to the river is at the county road crossing about a mile upstream from where Kent Creek flows into the Frio. US 83 crosses a mile north of Leakey. The East Frio River adds its volume to the flow about a half mile downstream with FM 337 crossing 1.5 miles farther down one mile east of Leakey.

There is a private camp about a mile south of Leakey off FM 1120 with about a mile of shoreline and camping facilities available. Another private camp is located a mile downstream with a half mile of shoreline and camping facilities available. Two miles down from the FM 337 crossing is that of FM 1120; it crosses again 4 miles downriver at Rio Frio. FM 1050 crosses 2 miles downstream and 1.5 miles above Garner State Park just off US 83 some 22 miles north of Uvalde. The river borders the east boundary of the park for 1.5 miles. Complete camping facilities are available here. A low water dam is located within the park named for the popular Vice-Pres. John Nance Garner.

Magers Crossing off FM 1050 is 1.5 miles downstream from the park with another private park located another mile downriver with camping facilities available. The only serious natural hazard along the river is a waterfall located some 4 miles below the dam in Garner State Park. The falls can be run during high water, but extreme caution should be used. Take a good look before you try it!

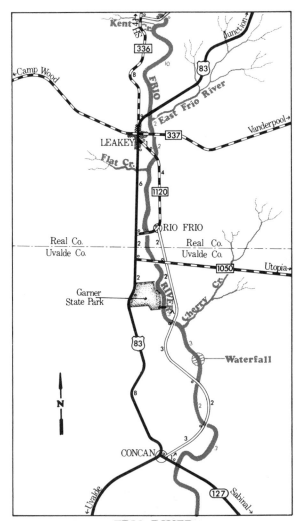

FRIO RIVER
KENT CREEK TO CONCAN
31 Miles

A county road off SH 127 crosses a couple of times before the highway itself crosses one mile east of Concan. It is about 9 miles from the park to this last crossing.

From here on the Frio River winds through semi-arid ranching country where at times the stream bed is completely dry. In general, the lower sections of the river are not suitable for recreational use except during flood conditions, and then they become hazardous for most activities. One of Texas' newer lakes is the Choke Canyon Reservoir, a 27,000-acre impoundment west of Three Rivers. Boat ramps and camping facilities are available, thus greatly expanding the recreational opportunities on this lower portion of the Frio. The State Park headquarters is located at the South Shore Unit off State Highway 72 west of Three Rivers. Adequate water is found below the confluence of the Frio with the Atascosa and the Nueces near Three Rivers.

Guadalupe River

Before we begin sounding like a chamber of commerce telling of the beauty and outstanding recreational opportunities afforded by the Guadalupe River, let's listen to some of the warnings given by some folks who should know, the water safety officials of the Texas Parks and Wildlife Department.

While agreeing that it is a beautiful river, they say that the portion below Canyon Dam is the deadliest 25 miles in Texas amid scenery which belies the danger of the river's swift waters. They say that visitors to this compellingly beautiful area often seem to be so captivated that they abandon all concern for safety. A vast flotilla of all kinds of water craft can be seen shooting the rapids during the warm-weather months, even during high flow periods when many expert canoeists avoid the river.

For example, an estimated 250,000 persons visited the Lower Guadalupe during the Fourth of July weekend in 1981, and a large percentage of those were on the river as waders, swimmers, inner-tubers, or operators of small craft.

The river claimed 14 lives in 1981, but the water safety officials were surprised that the toll was not higher. According to the water safety program director, J. Palmer, "Recreationists are using a treacherous river like an amusement park, without realizing the potential danger."

The Memorial Day weekend in 1981 is a good example of the mayhem which has become commonplace on the river. Red Cross volunteers from Houston and Dallas pulled between 600 and 700 persons from the swift waters in two days, and many of these were on the verge of drowning when help arrived. Hundreds were treated for injuries at temporary aid stations.

The temperament of the river in this stretch below Canyon Dam is entirely dependent upon the water releases. It can be fairly tame when those releases are 750 cubic feet per second or lower. However, heavy rains on the watershed have forced the

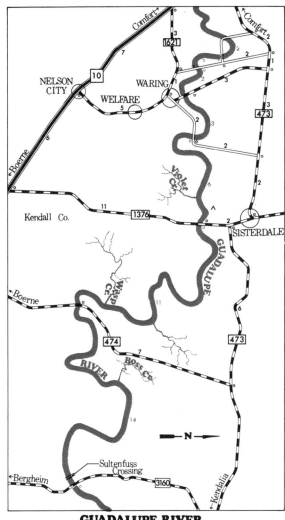

GUADALUPE RIVER
Waring to FM 3160
39 Miles

U.S. Army Corps of Engineers to increase the flow to as much as 5,000 cubic feet per second, a rate which makes any form of whitewater sport extremely dangerous.

Regardless of the state of the river, officials urge all prospective river floaters to use a personal floatation device (life vest) whenever they are on the water. By all means, check the water flow and stay off the river if it is too swift. Many newspapers publish river flow information each Friday with release rates coded according to the relative safety for floaters.

It should be noted that drinking and drugs also are factors which have contributed to many drowning deaths in the Guadalupe. Intoxication increases the chances of a spill in rough water and reduces the percentage of survival once in the water. Be a teetotaler while on the river!

Information on the river flow can be obtained by calling the U.S. Corps of Engineers at Canyon Dam at 512/964-3341 or by contacting any of the many canoe rental-outfitters in the area you wish to visit.

Now that you have been forewarned about the dangers of this beautiful and exciting river, let's take a look at its many recreational possibilities.

With north and south prongs rising in the west central part of Kerr County, the spring-fed Guadalupe flows eastward through the Hill Country until it issues from the Balcones Escarpment near New Braunfels. From here it meanders through the coastal plain to San Antonio Bay, a total distance of some 250 miles. Joined by the Comal River, the San Marcos River, and the San Antonio River, the combined total runoff exceeds a million acre-feet annually. The name Guadalupe is derived from Nuestra Senora de Guadalupe, the name given the stream by Alonso de Leon.

Several lakes have been created on the river including Canyon Reservoir, the major one, and six smaller ones, Lake McQueeney, Lake Dunlap, Lake Placid, Lake Gonzales, Wood Lake, and Meadow Lake. The water flow on portions of the river is controlled by the release through the dams, especially that section below Canyon Dam. Generally, there is enough water for recreational use on the entire river with the exception of the extreme upper reaches. Here the river is very narrow and shallow, and conditions are not conducive to recreational use until it reaches the vicinity of Comfort and Waring.

Kerrville State Park is located on the upper section just below the confluence of the two forks. A series of eight small low-water dams that do not seriously restrict water flow are located between

Distribute weight and gear evenly for a safe and comfortable trip.

Kerrville and Comfort. Below the sixth dam about 2 miles above Comfort, there is a mill channel with a 10-foot waterfall.

Your highway map may not show the community of Waring, but it is located on FM 1621 between IH 10 and FM 473 east of Comfort. The 39-mile section from here down to the crossing of FM 3160 is considered an excellent one for recreational use. The river is very scenic with high limestone bluffs and typical Edwards Plateau vegetation lining the banks. There are many small rapids to lend excitement to the floater, yet there are only a few potentially dangerous places. Limbs and brush hanging out over the river can be a problem as can several low-water crossings. Camping areas are a problem since there aren't many sand and gravel bars that lend themselves to camping and day use. Again be reminded that trespassers are not welcome on the banks!

Beginning at the county road crossing off FM 473 some 4 miles northwest of Waring, the river normally is not passable beneath the bridge, but there is access for a put-in. The same road crosses 2 miles downriver, and this low-water crossing also prevents passage beneath the bridge. There is danger of being swept under these low-water bridges, so anytime you find one, be very cautious, and take out in plenty of time to portage around if necessary. The next county road crossing is one mile downstream; at last report, this is just a ford rather than a bridge, and shallow water could require a walk-through.

It is another 2 miles to the next county road crossing just north of Waring. At low water levels, the river is passable beneath the bridge here. If there is any doubt, take a close look before going under.

For someone not familiar with this section of the Guadalupe, it might be well to check the river flow by the river gauge that is located at the north end of the low-water bridge southeast of Comfort. If the gauge reads below the 5-foot mark, the river will be shallow. If it reads near or over the 7-foot mark, the river is high and should be considered dangerous.

Another county road off FM 473 crosses at a spot known as Zoeller's Crossing about 3 miles down. This one is passable beneath the bridge at low water levels. A private camp is located on the left bank some 5 miles below this crossing. Only picnic tables are available, and there is a small fee for camping. The campground can be reached via a private road off RR 1376, some 3 miles south of Sisterdale. RR 1376 crosses the river a mile below the camp.

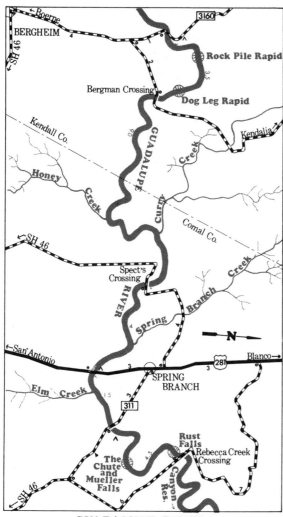

GUADALUPE RIVER
FM 3160 to Rebecca Creek Crossing
22.4 Miles

The next road crossing is 11 miles to FM 474 some 7 miles north of Boerne. Known as Ammans Crossing, this can be an alternate launch or take-out point for a shorter float. The next 14 miles down to the crossing of FM 3160 would be a good choice. Access to the river here is on the road right-of-way down the steep bank on the north side of the river. Just above this crossing is what is known as the old Sultenfuss crossing that has been closed off to the public. It is named after one of the first white settlers of the region.

The 22-mile section of the Guadalupe from FM 3160 to the Rebecca Creek crossing, the last road crossing above Canyon Reservoir, is considered one of the most scenic stretches of river in all of Texas and has been the subject of very intense study by the Texas Parks and Wildlife Department as published in their *Pathways and Paddleways*. This study was first published in August of 1971, and

even though the recommended "Guadalupe Waterway" has never been established for a number of reasons, most of the data collected about the river itself is still current.

There are at least 55 rapids of various classes scattered throughout this stretch, most of which are navigable and will cause few problems for recreationists. There are four areas that can be dangerous and require careful inspection before attempting a run. The first is the Rock Pile Rapid and is located about a mile below the FM 3160 crossing. The many large, closely spaced rocks create a challenge to even an experienced canoeist. The second danger spot is called the Dog Leg Rapid, so called because the channel makes a sharp turn to the right in conjunction with a very steep gradient. This one is 3 miles below the FM 3160 crossing.

The third serious obstacle is Mueller Falls located about 1.5 miles below the FM 311 crossing. The danger factor rises as the water level rises. The Falls are always dangerous, but there is a chute to the left of the island that offers an exciting run through fast water with a series of baldcypress trees in the middle of the channel. The fourth and last major problem area is Rust Falls located about a quarter of a mile above the Rebecca Creek Crossing. These falls, too, are very dangerous, but the experienced and adventuresome can run the passageway through a small chute to the left of the falls near the baldcypress trees in the river.

For those who do not feel that they have the experience to run these danger spots, all can be safely and rather easily portaged. As they say, sometimes discretion is the better part of valor! Don't take any unnecessary chances.!

Now that you've been forewarned about the worst, let's go back to that FM 3160 crossing and move downstream, taking a look at the various crossings and campsites to be found along the way. Access to the river is available at this crossing on the road right-of-way by a steep bank on the north side or through the private canoe camp adjacent to the bridge on the north bank. The study conducted by the Texas Parks and Wildlife Department contained plans for a primitive camp to be called River Bend Canoe Camp at a point just above the Rock Pile Rapids where the bluffs pull away from the river on the right to create suitable terrain for camping. There is also a convenient gravel bar above the rapids for beaching your canoe and preplanning your route.

When the water is high, two large boulders some 10 feet from the right bank and about 4 feet apart allow room for a canoe to pass between them. During low water conditions, passage may be found through a channel about 5 yards from the left bank. If you are in doubt of your ability to handle your craft, always portage or line it through. About 100 yards below the Rockpile is a small rapid that requires a quick left turn in low water. A bit farther down is another area that requires skillful steering due to the numerous rocks in the channel where the river makes a definite bend to the right and turns south.

Dog Leg Rapid with its 45 degree turn to the right has a steep gradient (a 6-foot drop) that is easily noted and requires skillful handling to safely negotiate. Take time to look it over!

The next crossing is known as Bergman crossing, so named after the original land owner, about .8 mile below the Dog Leg and 3.4 miles below the FM 3160 crossing. At normal water level or below, the river is passable beneath the bridge, but be careful if the level is a bit high. It's a good idea to beach above the bridge and portage around. Also, logs and brush piled against the bridge can increase the danger.

Some 20 minutes down from this crossing is an area where a canoe camp was planned as a part of the Guadalupe Waterway by the Texas Parks and Wildlife Department. A grove of native pecans across the river from a myriad of springs was to be the site of "The Springs" canoe camp, an ideal spot for the first night's camp of a weekend trip. Keep in mind, however, that the planned waterway has not materialized, and the land is still privately owned.

In the 9 miles to the next county road crossing, two large creeks enter the river. At Honey Creek, the water runs into the river from a slab of limestone which is so smooth and flat that it resembles a slab of poured concrete. The wide channel of Curry Creek is navigable for about a mile upstream to where the creek changes from a quiet hollow to a series of pools and falls. Lily pads, Spanish moss, and palmettoes give one the impression of a lazy, East Texas bayou. The major campground of the planned waterway would have been just above Curry Creek with both group and individual campsites.

Specht's crossing is at a county road 3 miles west of Spring Branch. At normal level or below, the river is passable beneath the bridge. This is a good put-in or take-out point for a one-day trip.

About half-way to the next crossing, that of US 281, is another proposed canoe camp at the point where Spring Branch joins the river. The clear water of Spring Branch flows over fern-covered limestone ledges into pools five to six feet deep, pro-viding excellent swimming and fine fishing. There is a falls some 700 feet up the creek.

A private campground and the Guadalupe Canoe Livery is located at the US 281 crossing 3 miles south of the Spring Branch community. The high bridge across the river gives poor access from the road right-of-way. Just below the bridge there is a rapid with a waterfall near the right bank. About 50 yards below the bridge, go to the left of a small cypress tree to avoid the waterfall.

Access is available 1.5 miles downstream at the FM 311 crossing on the road right-of-way. There is also a private camp on a private road off FM 311 with camping facilities available. This is the last take-out before being committed to Mueller Falls and Rust Falls described earlier. It is just under 2 miles down to The Chute and Mueller Falls and about 2 miles farther to Rust Falls. Then it's only a short distance on to the Rebecca Creek Crossing at a county road 3 miles east of Spring Branch. The access here is not too good, but this is the last crossing above the backwaters of Canyon Reservoir another 4 miles downriver.

And now we come to that section of the river below Canyon Dam that was mentioned earlier and described as the deadliest 25 miles in Texas. Perhaps that is partly because it is one of the most heavily used areas of any river in the state. The entire river area has been subjected to intense development with many subdivisions and camps, reducing the number of natural areas still to be found along its course.

The flow of the river here is dependent on the release of water from Canyon Dam. When the release is between 100 and 300 cubic feet per second, the river is navigable but shallow in places. From 400 to 600 cubic feet per second, the rapids require more skill and care to safely negotiate, and the hydraulic currents below the low-water dams become dangerous. Above the 600-cubic-feet-per-second release, the rapids and hydraulics are such that only the experienced should attempt them. However, for real excitement and uninterrupted flow, the optimum release is between the 600- and 900-cubic-feet-per-second mark. Anything above that is extremely dangerous. All safety precautions should be observed at all times along this stretch of the Guadalupe.

Along with the several low-water dams and many rapids along this stretch, there are two major waterfalls, Horseshoe Falls and Slumber Falls. Horseshoe Falls is never, I repeat *never*, passable as the river plunges over a horseshoe-shaped ridge and crashes about six or eight feet downward creating a very strong undertow. Slumber Falls can

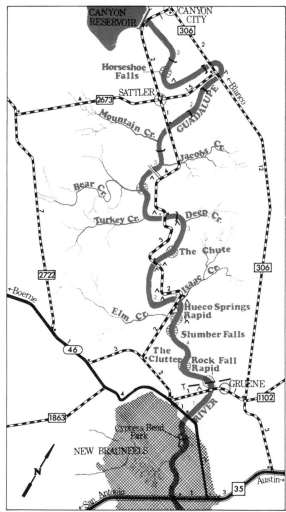

GUADALUPE RIVER
Canyon Dam to New Braunfels
24 Miles

is located here. Theirs is a complete canoe livery offering both kayaks and canoes as well as rafts and even innertubes! With some 500 acres, their facilities are complete with campground, screened-in cabins for eight, and a large vacation house furnished for eight. Their half mile of river frontage is ideal for rainbow trout fishing; they even offer day hunting for deer and turkey in season! And besides, they're fine folks with a lot of helpful information.

The River Road crossing on a county road off FM 2673 is 2 miles down. The two low-water dams just below FM 306 can be on the dangerous side with strong hydraulic currents if the water flow is nearing the 500-cubic-feet-per-second mark or above. The dam on below the River Road does not have the hydraulic currents of the first two, but it can be rough on your equipment.

The old River Road crosses the Guadalupe four or five times above the city of New Braunfels and there is another private road crossing where you must get permission for access. There are several private camps scattered along the river itself that offer a wide variety of camping facilities for a fee. No attempt will be made to list them all, but except on the most crowded holiday weekends, you should be able to find what you are looking for.

The greatest hazards on the river, for me, are the crowds of other recreationists on this heavily used section of the river, but there are several rapids that can cause trouble for the novice and for the foolhardy. The Devil's Playground Rapid near the junction with Bear Creek has no dangerous currents or rocks, but canoes seem to like to overturn here! Bad Rock Rapid, about a half mile downstream and so named because the rock sitting in midstream is a good (or perhaps I should say "bad") place to wrap a canoe. Run this one to the extreme right or left, staying away from the rock. The Chute actually bypasses a dam and offers an exciting channel of white water.

The Hueco (pronounced "Waco") Springs Rapid is a rough one, and if you run it, stay as close to the left bank as possible. I suggest you take a look first. Slumber Falls, a few hundred yards downstream, has already been described as having the worst hydraulic currents on the entire river. Go back and re-read about it! The Clutter, also known as Cypress Rapid, is best described as a "clutter" of cypress trees in the river, but there is a swift and narrow channel along the right bank. The Rock Fall Rapid just above the Gruene Crossing on the county road between FM 306 and SH 46 a mile north of New Braunfels is a jumble of boulders with no definite channel. Probably, the greatest

be run by the experienced canoeist by shooting the top portion of the rapid on the extreme right, going over the falls dead center and parallel to the river, paddling hard! Slumber Falls is said to have the worst hydraulic current on the entire river, so be careful!

We'll take a closer look at some of the most important rapids as we come to them moving downstream from the first launching point immediately below the dam. A road to the left of a hill will take you down to the river just below the spillway. Horseshoe Falls is about 1.5 miles downstream, so remember, do not try to run it! Portage on the left!

The first crossing of FM 306 is 3 miles from the launching point. The bridge is high, but there are concrete steps leading down to the water. The river then makes a loop of one mile coming back to the same highway. Ellen and Edward Martin's Whitewater Sports (512/964-3800 or 512/964-3371)

danger here isn't the rapids but the low-water crossing at the bridge. If the flow is above 500 cubic feet per second, a canoe cannot pass under. After working your way through the rapids, move into the large eddy on the right and portage around the bridge.

The SH 46 crossing is only another mile below this crossing and is near the northern city limits of New Braunfels. Cypress Bend Park, a city park in New Braunfels offers a mile of shoreline and a fine public campground with adequate facilities. There is a nominal charge in the park on weekends. The Comal River, known as the "shortest river in Texas", joins the Guadalupe from the right after traveling only 2.5 miles from its source, Comal Springs. These springs have the largest flow of any in the state, an average of 303 cubic feet per second. Actually, the river is the shortest in the nation with an equivalent water flow. This river may be explored upstream from the Guadalupe, and several private camps are located along the way.

The final road crossing on this section of the Guadalupe is at IH 35 one mile downstream from where the Comal River adds its considerable flow. There is a Texas Parks and Wildlife Department boat ramp beneath the highway.

The Guadalupe River, famous for its exciting whitewater challenge along its upper course, now begins to change to a twisting, turning, coastal river, leaving behind the scenic limestone bluffs so characteristic of the upper sections. The river is slow moving with no rapids of any importance, but with adequate water flow even during the dry season. The major problems for the floater consist of log jams and some small dams. There are six small reservoirs located in Guadalupe and Gon-

zales Counties, but the river is still suitable below these. Access is no problem because of several road crossings, but keep in mind that the shoreline is mostly privately owned, so get permission before even putting a foot out of your craft!

Here are four suggested sections of the lower Guadalupe that might be of interest to you. (1) A 21-mile section from Independence Park in Gonzales to the US 183 crossing 9 miles west of Yoakum. (2) A 30-mile stretch from the US 183 crossing to Cuero. (3) A 35-mile section from Cuero to the crossing of FM 447 southwest of Nursery. There is a potentially hazardous rapid about 3 miles above this crossing so be on the lookout for it. The river tumbles over a rock shelf and between some big rocks. A portage is no problem, or you may want to line your canoe through. (4) A 20-mile section from the FM 447 crossing to the City Park in Victoria. There are public camp sites within the park, and the area below most of the road crossings offers some camping space, but there are no facilities.

Below Victoria, the Guadalupe flows southerly to the Gulf and enters San Antonio Bay near the north end. The San Antonio River unites with the Guadalupe just a few miles upstream from where it flows into the Bay.

While the Guadalupe offers exciting but potentially hazardous canoeing and rafting opportunities, I consider the river's most attractive feature to be its outstanding fishing possibilities. The same section of river labeled the "deadliest 25 miles in Texas" has also produced the Texas state record for rainbow trout. Virginia Ann Ransleben of San Antonio caught a 4-pound, 13-ounce rainbow on April 17, 1982, while bank fishing using salmon eggs for bait.

The double-bladed paddle makes a kayak easier to propel and control, which is why this craft is especially popular with whitewater enthusiasts.

The Texas Parks and Wildlife Department began the put-and-take trout fishery here in the Guadalupe River back in 1966, a program which has spread to several other locations over the state. So, contrary to a local chamber of commerce brochure that claims this is "the only place in Texas where anglers can catch the magnificent rainbow trout," there are several other places such as the Brazos below Possum Kingdom, Forest Park near San Angelo, Boykin Springs near Jasper, and Rita Blanca Reservoir in the Panhandle, where an angler can have that chance.

The tackle used by fishermen will vary according to personal preference. Trout can be caught on a rod and reel with a light line and a small hook as well as with a fly rod. Ultralight spinning gear and small spinner baits work well. Even the simple pole and line baited with the salmon eggs, worms, or canned whole kernel corn works successfully. Some say the corn is the best of the baits for the hatchery-raised trout that are stocked at regular intervals during the winter months. The daily bag limit on rainbow trout is 5 and the possession limit is 10.

Still another trout record is claimed for this section of the Guadalupe River below Canyon Dam; a new record and a new category was established in the state fish record book when W. B. Trussell of Houston caught a 6½-pound German brown trout here on December 29, 1978. The fish also gave encouragement to the Texas Parks and Wildlife Department biologists and to members of Trout Unlimited, Inc., whose cooperative efforts were responsible for several years of stocking browns in the river.

In addition to the trout fishing, the Guadalupe is often referred to as the angler's supermarket where a fisherman can expect to catch striped bass, walleye, largemouth bass, spotted bass, smallmouth bass, and a variety of sunfish all in the same stream. And I know a lot of fishermen who make several trips each year half way across the state just to get in on the fine catfishing the river affords! Granted that the lower sections of the river have the most appeal for the catfisherman, this potential mixed bag is definitely a possibility for the fisherman who doesn't mind the heavy traffic of canoeists and rafters going by!

According to Bob Bounds, inland fisheries management coordinator for the Texas Parks and Wildlife Department, "There may be another river in these United States where you can catch such a variety of fish, but I certainly haven't heard about it!"

While the picturesque Guadalupe is thought by some to be the state's best put-and-take rainbow trout fishery, its sometimes swift currents and limited access keep fishermen from putting much of a dent in the population of the other sport fishes in the river. Before the construction of the Canyon Lake Dam, the river had populations of sunfish, catfish, largemouth black bass, and the Guadalupe spotted bass (a subspecies found only in Central Texas river systems). Shortly after the lake was impounded in the mid-1960s, the department began stocking rainbows in the swift and cold tailrace waters below the dam.

At the same time, Canyon Lake became the recipient of generous stockings of smallmouth bass, walleyes, and striped bass. These fish have exceeded expectations by growing, and in the case of smallmouths and walleyes, by reproducing. Natural reproduction of the stripers is suspected, but has not yet been confirmed. A sizeable number of the lake-stocked fish have made it through the dam and into the river below.

The mix of these species in the river has not caused a problem in the narrow confines of the river due to the fact that each has gravitated to a particular habitat type. The trout stick to the riffles and swift areas, stripers and walleyes like the deep pools, and the bass tend to find the eddy areas where overhanging trees provide shade. There are even differences in the habitat preference of the three bass species. The largemouths like shallow, shaded areas close to the bank while spotted bass venture into swifter water toward mid-stream. Smallmouths like to hug the bottom in pools and eddies where there is plenty of rock and rubble.

A canoe or flatbottom boat is almost a necessity to fish along stretches of the Guadalupe although there are fairly extensive areas which can be wade-fished. Be sure to keep in mind that while the riverbed is public property, most of the shoreline is private and subject to trespass laws. This is true throughout the entire length of the river. If you don't have permission, stay off the banks! Many landowners do have posted signs on their property, and some are said to back up their signs with loaded shotguns! Many of them claim to have had trouble from drunks, thieves, and rowdies; to them, everyone who comes to the area is an undesirable! After seeing and hearing how some folks act with regards to the property of others, I can't say that I blame them!

And there you have the Guadalupe River! What else can I say? As a recreational river, it has a great deal to offer no matter what your favorite water sport may be. If you don't mind the crowds you're likely to encounter, get with it! If you're lucky, maybe you can be there when it isn't so crowded.

The Lampasas River

From its headwaters in western Hamilton County, the Lampasas flows 100 miles southeast through Lampasas, Burnet, and Bell counties to unite with the Leon River and form the Little River just south of Belton. Recreational use on the upper portion flowing through the rugged hill country is restricted, due to the usually low water level. However, the picture changes during periods of heavy rain when the river becomes an exciting corridor through a scenic and interesting area.

The first 47-mile section of the river that is worth investigation during a period of high water begins at the crossing of FM 1047 in the southwestern edge of Hamilton County and goes to the crossing of Ranch Road 580 about 10 miles northeast of Lampasas. US 84, US 281, and RR 1690 along with several county roads cross the river with varying degrees of access to the river. At the RR 580 crossing, there is approximately 50 feet of shoreline available on the right-of-way.

The next 42-mile section of the Lampasas River extends from this crossing on RR 580 near Rumley in Lampasas County to the FM 2484 crossing near Youngsport about 11 miles south of Killeen. Again the river passes through typical hill country terrain, and during the high-water periods, many small rapids add interest and excitement. While there are numerous public road crossings through this stretch, some of these are fenced making access to the river difficult. To be on the safe side, always ask for permission before climbing any fence!

The first crossing is that of RR 2313 about 5 miles north of Kempner where there is reported to be about 50 feet of shoreline available on the highway right-of-way. The US 190 crossing one mile west of Kempner also offers 50 feet of shoreline in the highway right-of-way. There are two county road crossings along here, and FM 963 crosses about a mile north of the small town of Okalla. Steep banks at the FM 440 crossing near the community of Ding Dong make access at this point difficult. FM 2484

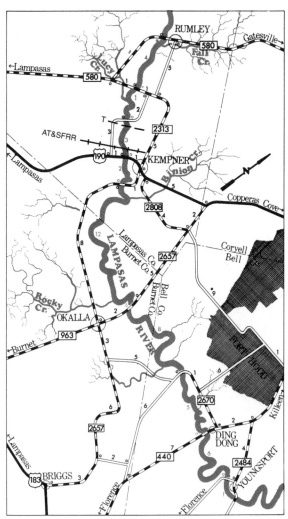

LAMPASAS RIVER
Rumley to Youngsport
42 Miles

then crosses at Youngsport; the headwaters of Stillhouse Hollow Reservoir begin just below this crossing.

The 17.5 miles of the Lampasas River below the Stillhouse Hollow Dam and the junction with the Leon River can be a pleasant one-day trip when the water flow is sufficient. This is dependent entirely on the release of water from the dam. A flow of between 200 and 300 cubic feet per second is the optimum level for safe recreational use. There are no public camp sites in this area, and there are few natural camp sites along the river.

FM 1670 crosses the river immediately below the Stillhouse Hollow Dam. The IH 35 crossing is about 4 miles downstream where a good road for easy access leads down to the river at this point. A county road crosses about a half mile below this point, and another county road off FM 436 crosses 5 miles farther down. FM 1123 crosses 4 more miles downriver at a point about 3 miles southeast of Belton. The last crossing on the Lampasas before it joins the Leon River is that of a county road off FM 436 some 5 miles from Belton. It is about a half mile below this crossing that the two rivers unite to form the Little River.

Information on the flow of this section can be obtained by calling the Corps of Engineers at Stillhouse Hollow Dam at 817/939-2461.

As for the fishing in Stillhouse Hollow Reservoir and the river itself, thanks to the efforts of the Texas Parks and Wildlife Department, it is better known for its smallmouth bass fishing than for largemouth. Smallmouth bass were first stocked in 1974, and natural reproduction has been confirmed in the clear water and rocky shorelines of the lake. Walleye and hybrid stripers have also been stocked and are reportedly doing well. The upper reaches of the lake offer good fishing for catfish, too.

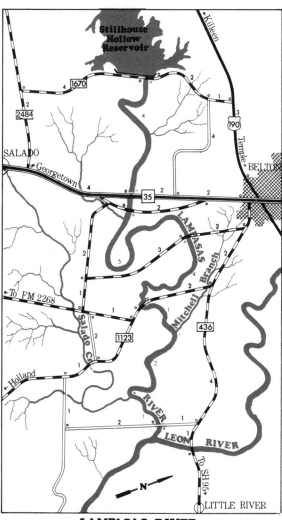

LAMPASAS RIVER
Stillhouse Hollow Reservoir
to Leon River
17.5 Miles

Canoeing offers one of the most rewarding ways to explore the remaining untouched Texas wilderness.

Lavaca River

From its beginning northwest of Hallettsville to the point where it enters Lavaca Bay on the Gulf of Mexico, the Lavaca River is a typical coastal river with its flow being determined entirely by runoff. As a result, the upper reaches of the river do not have sufficient water levels for recreation except during periods of flooding. Since the river is not spring fed and the watershed is rather small, the portion of the river in Lavaca County is seasonal. The stretch that is most likely to be suitable for recreational use begins near the Navidad Community at a road crossing off FM 822 some 9 miles northwest of Edna. The course of the river lies within the coastal plain, and the vegetation on the banks is composed of typical coastal hardwoods. Log and brush jams can create a problem for the floater.

This 25.5-mile section of the Lavaca River extends down to the Old Vanderbilt Park just below FM 616 near the junction of the Lavaca and Navidad Rivers. From here, it is about 5 or 6 miles up the Navidad River to the Lake Texana Dam. Lake Texana is the new name for the old Palmetto Bend Lake.

For a shorter float, there are four road crossings in between that can be utilized for putting in or taking out. A second county road off FM 822 crosses 7 miles downstream at a point about 3 miles northwest of Edna. The next is at the US 59 crossing 4 miles down the river and about 1 mile west of Edna. Three river miles will get you to the county road between FM 234 and FM 1822; another 4 miles finds a county road that also connects these same two highways. Then it's 7 more miles to the FM 616 crossing and 0.5 mile on to the Old Vanderbilt Park on the east bank. Good river access is available here at this point.

The Lavaca River empties into Lavaca Bay on the Gulf about 10 miles downstream from this point. This is the main reason that the river is considered

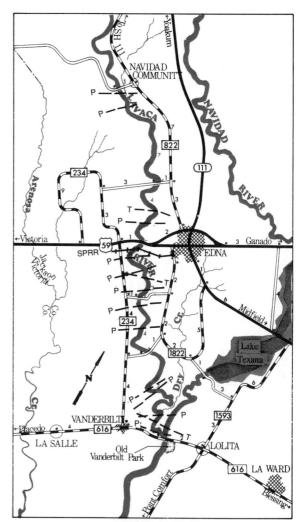

LAVACA RIVER
Navidad Community Crossing to
Old Vanderbilt Park
25.5 Miles

a primary stream in the state; the fact that it does flow directly into the Gulf, the principle stream to do so between the Guadalupe and the Colorado. The Spanish called it the Lavaca (meaning "cow") River because of the many bison to be found in the area at that time.

Its sister stream and principle tributary, the Navidad River, will not be considered in this text since its primary recreational attraction is now Lake Texana, an 11,000-acre impoundment that not only provides recreational and fishing opportunities but also a dependable municipal and industrial water supply for the area. (See *A Guide to Fishing in Texas* Lone Star Books, Houston Texas, for more on this one!)

Leon River

The Leon River originates in Eastland County when its three forks, the North, Middle, and South, come together for the 185-mile trip to the southeast to unite with the Lampasas River to form the Little River. And while these upper reaches do not have sufficient water for recreational use except during periods of heavy rainfall, the lower sections do have enough water for use most of the time as they flow through a scenic portion of the Cross Timbers area of Central Texas.

There are two reservoirs located in the upper section of the Leon River. The first is Lake Leon, a 1,500-acre reservoir just a few miles south of IH 20 between Ranger and Eastland. Considered by some as a "country club" lake, it does have marina facilities for boaters and fishermen. The second is Lake Proctor, a 4,600-acre lake built by the U.S. Army Corps of Engineers, with plenty of facilities around the lake to accommodate even the heavy weekend traffic. The 31-mile section of the river between these two lakes is extremely narrow and shallow, making it impractical for use as a recreational river.

That section of the river below Lake Proctor can be suitable for recreational use, but only when water is being released from the dam and after heavy rains. Depending on the amount of the flow, there can be some small rapids along the way. As on all rivers in this section of the state, about the only problems will be occasional log jams.

Although we do not have this section mapped for you, there are many road crossing access points from below Proctor Dam all the way to Gatesville. Also there are two private camps in the vicinity of Hamilton. The Texas Highway Department's county road maps for Comanche, Hamilton, and Coryell Counties will be of tremendous help in locating these crossings and other features of the river.

The first crossing below Proctor Dam is that of US 67 some 8 miles northeast of Comanche. In ad-

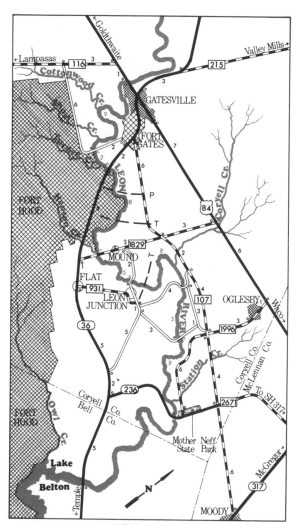

LEON RIVER
US 84 to Mother Neff State Park
46 Miles

dition to the several county road crossings along the way, the river is crossed by FM 1476, FM 1702, US 281 about 5 miles north of Hamilton, SH 22 some 6 miles east of Hamilton, SH 36 one mile west of Jonesboro, and US 84 in the western city limits of Gatesville.

The 46-mile section of the Leon River from this point in Gatesville down to the Mother Neff State Park above Lake Belton usually has enough water flow for recreational use except during very dry periods. A number of creeks join the river along the way to add to the flow through the rather steep and muddy banks lined with elm, willow, and sycamore. The US 84 crossing is a good point to begin a float that will carry you through some scenic vistas of oak- and cedar-covered hills. Occasional log jams may be encountered, and the lower portion does become rather sluggish as you approach the backwaters of Lake Belton.

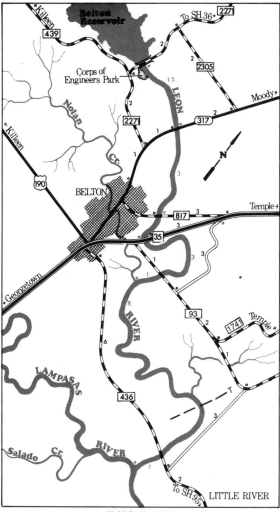

LEON RIVER
Belton Reservoir to
Lampasas River
17.5 Miles

The next crossing is that of a county road off SH 36 four miles south of Gatesville some 9 miles downriver. SH 36 crosses another 2 miles downstream, and FM 1829 crosses 8 river-miles down. It should be noted that the right bank of the river from this county road down to FM 1829 is a part of the Fort Hood Reservation. A county road off FM 931 crosses at a point one mile west of the community of Leon Junction. Two other county roads

cross the river in the 13-mile stretch above the crossing of SH 236 and Mother Neff State Park. Camping and picnic facilities are available here at the park.

Below this point, you enter the upper section of Lake Belton. Built in 1954 by the U.S. Army Corps of Engineers, the lake has provided outstanding fishing for both black and white bass. The more recent introduction of hybrid stripers has given a new dimension to fishing for local and visiting anglers. Catfish and crappie also entice fishermen to the lake.

For an easy float that can be enjoyed by the novice, the family, or a group, the 17.5-mile section from the Belton Dam down to the junction with the Lampasas River is a good choice provided the water release from the dam is in the vicinity of 300 cubic feet per second. The release is greater during periods of heavy rainfall, thus making recreational use of this portion of the Leon River more practical and enjoyable. The first couple of miles are scenic and variations in the gradient will create a few areas of fast water. The water quality itself does deteriorate below Belton as the river meanders slowly between the steep earthen banks. There are plenty of road crossings, but steep and sometimes muddy banks may make access difficult at some of these.

The best starting point is at the Corps of Engineers Park immediately below the dam. SH 317 crosses 1.5 miles downstream at a point 2 miles north of the city of Belton. FM 817 crosses near the northeastern city limits 3 miles farther down. Another mile gets you to the crossing of IH 35 between Belton and Temple. The next crossing, FM 1741, is after a wide loop of some 3 miles of river. If the upper portion of this section of the river is too low, this might be an alternate launching site. A short portage will be required since there is no direct access to the river from the road. The final crossing before the junction of the rivers is that of FM 436, some 9 miles downstream. The Leon and the Lampasas come together about a mile below this crossing. From this point on it becomes the Little River. Check elsewhere in this book for the recreational opportunities of the Little River.

For information on the river flow and water release from the Belton Dam, call 817/939-5251.

Little River

Formed by the junction of the Leon and the Lampasas Rivers southeast of Belton, it may be "little" when compared to some other Texas streams, but it is plenty big enough to offer fine recreational opportunities both before and after being joined by the San Gabriel River in Milam County. The Little River flows some 75 miles southeast and east to unite with the Brazos southwest of Hearne.

The first practical access is actually on the Leon River about a mile above the point where the Leon and the Lampasas join. This is at the FM 436 crossing some 5 miles southeast of Belton. A road beneath this bridge goes right down to the river. The next access is 7 miles downstream at the SH 95 crossing where again a road goes down beneath the bridge and about 50 feet of shoreline is available for public use. There are then 3 county road crossings scattered over the next 14 or 15 river miles, but at the last report, the bridges are washed out at all of them. The first is 3.5 miles below the SH 95 crossing; the second is 6 miles further; the third is yet another 4 miles. From this last one, another 5 miles will take you to the FM 437 crossing 15 miles west of Cameron. A road does go down to the river beneath the bridge, but access is poor.

This 25-mile section flows through mostly flat farming country with considerable vegetation along the steep earthen banks. Trees falling across the stream can create log jams that are a nuisance. It's a good idea to avoid this river at high water levels or during rainy periods.

The 33-mile stretch from the FM 437 crossing to the FM 1600 crossing lies entirely in Milam County. Again, log jams and the steep, muddy banks are about the only problems you're likely to encounter.

Five roads do cross the river through here, dividing it into relatively equal segments. The first of these is a county road off FM 437 some 7 miles

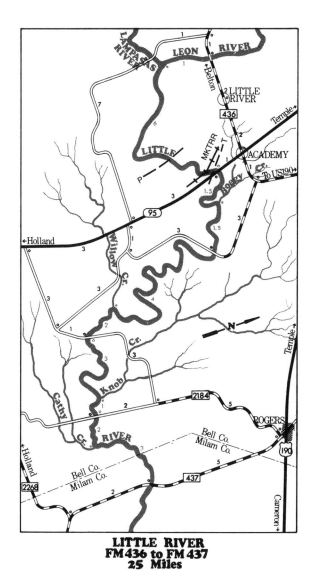

**LITTLE RIVER
FM 436 to FM 437
25 Miles**

downstream. The second is a county road off FM 485 at 10 more river miles. The third crossing between the point of origin and the last is at FM 486 another 8 miles down. From here it is 8 more river miles to the FM 1600 crossing where about one-half mile of shoreline is available on the highway right-of-way.

The next segment of the Little River is the 38 miles from the FM 1600 crossing to the Sugarloaf Mountain crossing off US 190 some 13 miles southeast of Cameron. Sugarloaf Mountain is a sandstone spire which rises above the surrounding countryside with variable banks of red, yellow and rust colors that are visible for miles.

The San Gabriel River enters the Little River from the right 3 miles below the FM 1600 crossing. This river, as well as the other two forks of the Little River, are covered elsewhere in the text.

The next road crossing is that of US 77-SH 36 one mile southeast of Cameron, about 10 miles past the junction of the San Gabriel. Two more miles will get you to the crossing of a county road off FM 2095. This is the last road access until the Sugarloaf Mountain crossing between Branchville on US 190 and Gause on US 79, some 23 miles downriver.

Seven miles further down is the point where the Little River flows into the Brazos River. Three miles downstream from this point is the crossing of US 79, a good takeout spot even in bad weather.

There are limited camping areas at most of these road crossings, but don't forget to get permission before camping in those places that are on private land. Quite often you can get permission by simply asking, but to camp without asking can make you the target for some landowner's wrath! And rightly so!

The smaller rivers such as this one may have obstacles not found on the larger streams, but I, for one, prefer them if they are big enough and clear enough for my canoe to pass through!

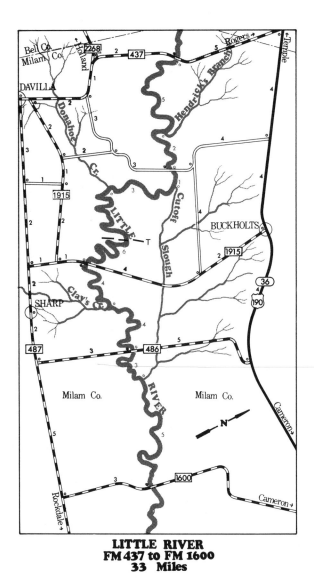

**LITTLE RIVER
FM 437 to FM 1600
33 Miles**

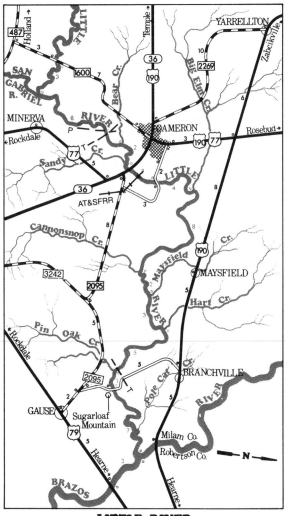

**LITTLE RIVER
FM 1600 to
Sugarloaf Mountain Crossing
38 Miles**

Llano River

The Llano River is formed near the town of Junction where the North and South Forks of the river unite to begin a 100-mile journey to the Colorado River and Lake L.B.J. It is a spring-fed stream widely known for its beauty as it travels through this section of the Hill Country. As with other rivers in this Edwards Plateau region, recreational use is at its best when the river is on a rise following moderate to heavy rainfall. The higher the water level, the more challenging the many rapids that are present. During times of normal or below normal water level, several shallow areas can be a problem.

The North Llano rises in central Sutton County east of Sonora, and its 40 miles are generally too shallow for any significant recreational use. The river will range in width from 20 to 50 feet wide. It winds through Sutton and Kimble Counties towards Junction and is crossed by US 290 four times along with several county road crossings. During a period of heavy runoff, it might be well to check this area out.

The South Llano is some 55 miles long from its origin in Edwards County, flowing northeastward into Kimble County. It is a scenic, spring-fed stream with an average flow of around 75 cubic feet per second. Still, there are shallow areas during periods of normal level. This one, too, offers the best conditions during the time of abundant rain when the river is on a slight rise.

One of the most scenic and popular sections of the South Llano is located near Telegraph where "700 springs" pour out of the high limestone bluffs. With short riffles, chutes, small rapids, and still pools, the water level is usually adequate in this area, but the flow is somewhat reduced within 5 or 6 miles of Telegraph.

US 377 crosses the South Llano three times prior to its union with the North Llano at Junction. There are also two county roads that cross it. Several private camps are located along the river in the

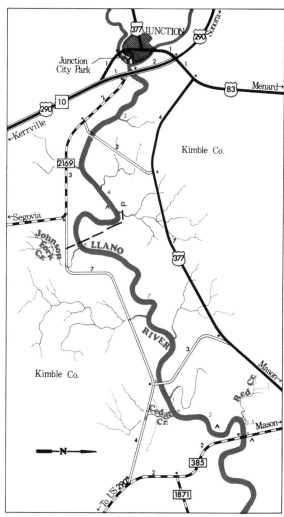

LLANO RIVER
Junction to FM 385
19 Miles

10-mile section southwest of Junction. Good access to the river is available at the Junction City Park on the City Lake.

The 19-mile section of the Llano River between Junction and the FM 385 crossing usually has sufficient water for recreational use as it moves slowly with no potential hazards or rapids. The countryside is typical Hill Country ranchland with yucca, cacti, mesquite, cedar, and live oak visible above the gently sloping banks. A small dam creates the Junction City Lake on the South Llano. Access is on the south side of the river below the dam with the North Llano entering on the left about a third of a mile downstream.

IH 10 crosses the river just one mile east of Junction, but there is no access here as the river is completely fenced off on all sides. There is a county road crossing 3 miles downstream between US 377 and FM 2169 at a point 2 miles east of Junction, but

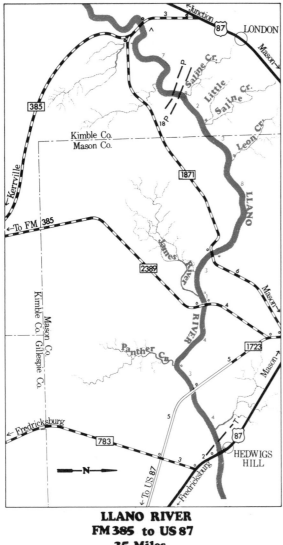

**LLANO RIVER
FM 385 to US 87
35 Miles**

Never underestimate currents; they are always stronger than they look.

the access here is very poor. A private camp located another 3 miles downriver off FM 2169 has about 2 miles of shoreline available with picnicking and camping facilities provided. Another county road off US 377 crosses 8 miles down with another private camp 3 miles past the crossing.

The crossing of FM 385 is about 20 miles northeast of Junction with a private camp immediately downstream. The camp does have about 3 miles of shoreline available, but there are no facilities for camping. All of these private camps along the river charge a nominal fee for launching or taking out as well as for leaving any vehicles there during a float.

The next 35-mile section of the Llano down to the crossing of US 87 also has good potential for recreational use as it travels through the ranchland setting of the Texas Hill Country in Kimble and

Mason Counties. Much of this area is highly prized for its whitetail deer hunting. Many times I've been on a deer stand within sight of the river and wished for a chance to float it!

The river is fairly broad and shallow with numerous stretches of calm, placid water at normal water levels. There are several cliffs along the way composed of layers of reddish-brown sandstone rock that rise 200 to 300 feet above the river. There will be an occasional gravel or sand bar that can be used for camping.

The first road crossing is that of FM 1871 some 20 miles downstream at a point 8 miles southwest of Mason. FM 2389 crosses another 4 miles downriver. There is a large island here that provides a good area for access, camping, and day use. It is 7 miles to the next crossing, a county road off FM 1723, but the access here is very poor. US 87 crosses 9 miles southeast of Mason at Hedwig's Hill.

From this crossing down to the city of Llano is a 30-mile stretch of the river that flows through a very scenic area, but the river must be on a rise or else passage will be difficult. The riverbed in some places may become as much as 100 yards wide, making the water extremely shallow. Also, large boulders and slabs of granite in the channel cause the stream to split into several channels with not enough water for recreational use during normal periods. Given a one- to two-foot rise, conditions become excellent for recreational use. The area is a part of what is known as the Llano Uplift, one of the most unique geologic features in the state. Some of the rocks which form the river bed are said to be one billion years old! There are many sand and gravel bars along this stretch that may be used for a lunch break or camping.

Access is no problem as there are several road crossings along the way. There is a private camp located about 10 miles downstream that offers a mile of shoreline. The camp is some 22 miles east of Mason off RR 152. The FM 2768 crossing is 2 miles below this camp and near the Mason-Llano County line. A county road between RR 152 and SH 29 crosses 5 miles downriver with another crossing 4 miles down at a point 8 miles west of Llano. The Robinson City Park off RR 152 in the western edge of Llano has about a mile of shoreline at the small 30-acre lake formed by a small dam. Picnicking facilities are provided, but no camping is allowed. A portage is necessary at this dam. SH 16 crosses in the city of Llano, but the high bridge here offers poor access to the river.

The 20-mile stretch from Llano down to Lake L.B.J. is very similar to that upriver. The river is wide, and in many places, large boulders will divide the flow into several small streams. During periods of high water, there will be many good rapids along this route. FM 3404 crosses the river just upstream from Kingsland and FM 2900 crosses about a mile above the junction with the Colorado River and the backwaters of Lake L.B.J.

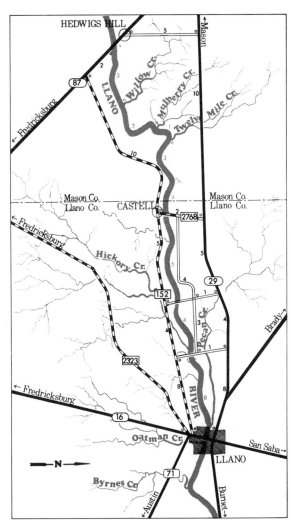

LLANO RIVER
US 87 to Llano
30 Miles

Sand and gravel bar camping provides a lot of fun and fellowship on an outing. Remember to carry out everything you carry in, including waste and garbage.

Llano River **43**

Medina River

With a total length of about 116 miles, the Medina River is formed by the junction of its North and West prongs near the town of Medina in Bandera County. A relatively small spring-fed river, the Medina normally has a sufficient flow for recreational use in the section from Medina down to Lake Medina below Bandera Falls. The water flows swiftly over a limestone bottom with numerous small rapids. By exercising due caution, none of these are considered dangerous at normal water levels. However, this section can be very dangerous as the water level increases during times of heavy runoff. In addition to the overhanging limbs, rocks, and cypress stands in the river, the many twisting white water chutes and small falls can be dangerous hazards, especially to the inexperienced.

Lake Medina, built in the early 1900s as a supply for irrigation water, produced a 13-pound, 8-ounce largemouth bass in 1943 that stood as the Texas state record for almost 37 years. The lake also provides catfish and crappie for area fishermen.

The 27-mile section of the Medina River from the Medina City Park down to Bandera Falls just above the lake is perhaps the best portion of the entire river for recreational use. The first access point is at Moffett Park, a city park located on the west side of the city of Medina. There is about 100 feet of shoreline available here. The first road crossing is a county road off SH 16 at the 2-mile point with SH 16 crossing a mile farther down. Four miles downstream is a private camp with about 2 miles of shoreline available. This camp does have camping and picnicking facilities.

At a point 5 miles east of Bandera, a county road off SH 16 crosses a mile below the camp. Four miles downriver, SH 16 again crosses the river 3 miles west of Bandera. A roadside park here provides about 100 feet of shoreline. Camping is allowed at the roadside parks, according to the latest reports. However, check to make sure there are

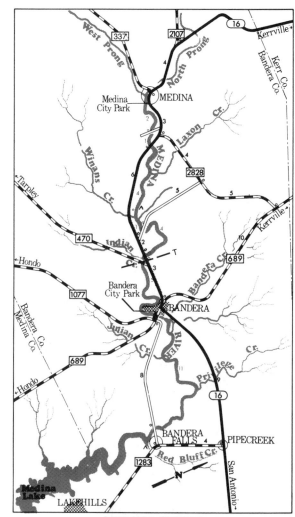

MEDINA RIVER
Medina City Park to
Bandera Falls
27 Miles

no signs that prohibit camping. The FM 470 crossing is only a half mile downstream with another roadside park offering 100 feet of shoreline.

Five miles downriver, the Hudspeth City Park located in the southwestern section of Bandera has about one-fourth mile of shoreline. A low-water dam forms a small lake at this point. Immediately below this dam FM 689 crosses in the city of Bandera. A road goes down to the river underneath the bridge. The city park is the usual takeout point for those not wishing to continue on down to Bandera Falls or into the lake.

A county road crosses 11 miles downstream at a point about one mile northwest of Bandera Falls. This is a low-water crossing that provides good access, but cars have to be parked on top of the hill.

There is a private camp another mile downstream just above the waters of Lake Medina and about a hundred yards up Red Bluff Creek with camping and picnicking facilities available.

The 64-mile section of the Medina River between the lake and the junction with the San Antonio River is a slow moving, meandering stream that is relatively narrow and shallow. While it has no rapids, there are numerous log jams that choke the river. There are road crossings that divide the river into segments from 0.5 to 5 miles in length, but in spite of this, this section of the river is just not suited to extensive recreational use

Food tastes better over an open fire, but never leave any sign of your fire behind you. Bury or carry out ashes and even resod if necessary to leave the wilderness as you found it.

Perhaps the most affordable recreational use of your nearest waterway lies in an afternoon of peaceful bank fishing.

Neches River

Named for the Neches Indians that lived along its banks, the river has a length of over 400 miles with normally abundant rainfall along its course. It enters Sabine Lake and the Gulf of Mexico just above Port Arthur with a flow of about 6 million acre-feet per year.

There are two major reservoirs in the watershed, Lake Palestine and B. A. Steinhagen (Dam "B") Reservoir, that are important recreational areas for fishing, boating, and camping. Much smaller Rhine Lake is located above Lake Palestine, and use of the river between these two and below Palestine is limited to periods of heavy runoff. Even then, the presence of numerous drifts and log jams can prohibit floating. These continue to be a problem as far down as Dam "B."

Flowing through typical East Texas pine and hardwood bottomlands, the narrow and shallow stream flows some 40 miles from Rhine Lake to Lake Palestine. The river is somewhat better suited for recreational use below the Lake Palestine Dam when water is being released in sufficient quantity. Two sections in this part that could be worth checking include the 24.5 miles from the US 175 crossing between Jacksonville and Frankston to the US 79 crossing southwest of Jacksonville (there is reportedly adequate shoreline available for public use along the right-of-way of US 175) and a 17-mile trip from the Brick Smith crossing 10 miles south of Maydelle off US 84 west of Rusk to the SH 21 crossing. Adequate shoreline is available for public use at both of these.

The 32-mile section between SH 21 and SH 7 is referred to as the Big Slough Trip. The Big Slough is a small channel that leads off from the Neches through the Davy Crockett National Forest to return some 4 miles downstream, making a loop waterway of about 8 miles. All of this has been marked as a canoe trail by the U.S. Forest Service, and the area has been considered a potential wilderness area.

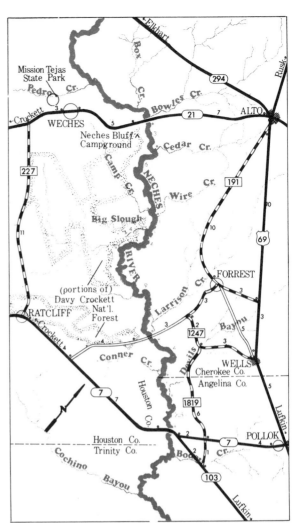

**NECHES RIVER
SH 21 to SH 7
32 Miles**

At the SH 21 crossing, there is about 100 yards of shoreline available for public use along the highway right-of-way. The Neches Bluff campground is a Forest Service campground located on a tall bluff on the right bank. Forest Road 511 leads off the highway to the campground about a mile below the crossing. The entrance to Big Slough is about 10 miles below the SH 21 crossing. A dirt road off Forest Road 511 also leads down to Big Slough. A county road off FM 1247 crosses the river about 8.5 miles above the SH 7 crossing. SH 7 and SH 103 cross the river some 26 miles southeast of Crockett. A Texas Parks and Wildlife Department boat ramp is located here for public use.

From this point, it is 42 miles on to the crossing of US 59 some 3 miles south of Diboll and the next boat ramp. SH 94 crosses the river 8 miles west of Lufkin but access here ranges from poor to non-ex-

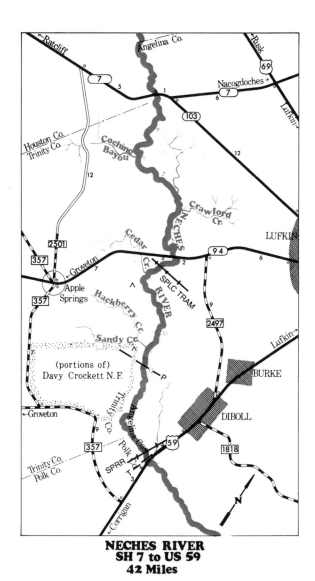

NECHES RIVER
SH 7 to US 59
42 Miles

NECHES RIVER
US 59 to US 69
44 Miles

istent. This is a very remote section through forest lands, and except for the driest summer months, there is usually enough water for floating in either a canoe or flat-bottomed john boat.

The 44-mile section from the US 59 crossing to the US 69 crossing between Woodville and Zavalla is very isolated with no crossings in between although there are a few private camps along the shore with dirt road access.

A friend and I were making this trip by canoe one fall when, it turned out, the water was just too low. We had allowed ourselves part of three days and two nights to make the trip, but by the end of the second day, we had made less than half of the distance. And since both of us could not take the extra time that the complete trip would have required, we had to take out at one of these camps.

The trip was still worthwhile and our campsite that first night was about as wild as they come! We

had stayed on the river until almost dark before pulling out and pitching our tent on kind of a "second bank." By the time we'd cooked and eaten the steaks we'd brought frozen from home and set out a short trotline across a bend of the river, we felt no need to be "rocked to sleep!" But a pack of coyotes, or what most East Texans call "wolves" set up a chorus nearby and managed to keep it up at intervals throughout the rest of the night!

The trotline produced two small channel cats the next morning which went into the ice chest to await some more of their kind. We did add one more that my buddy caught at noon while I fixed our lunch.

On a trip like this, I like to freeze water in clean milk cartons to carry along in the cooler. This way it serves as ice for cooling, and it's great drinking water as it melts. The days of drinking right from the river or stream in this part of the country are a thing of the past, I'm afraid. Good drinking water is one of the most important items; don't let yourself get caught as that author of old expressed, "Water, water everywhere, and not a drop to drink!"

Back to our problem on this portion of the Neches. The friend who recommended the float didn't tell me what time of the year he had breezed through, but early fall ain't the time! Too many trees down at water level! You don't go under or around; you go over! This is a condition that is fairly common on all the medium-sized rivers that flow through heavily forested areas. When the trees along the banks are tall enough to reach all the way across, look out!

About 7 miles above the US 69 crossing where Shawnee Creek enters the river is the site of old Fort Teran and an old ferry crossing. There is a dirt road that goes in to the spot from about halfway between Chester and Colmesneil. The condition of this road depends on local weather and rainfall, and as in most cases, the best bet is to inquire locally for directions or an alternate route if this one

is not passable. When conditions are favorable, this can be used for an access point for a shorter float.

Below the US 69 crossing, portions of the east bank are in the Angelina National Forest. The Bouton Lake Recreation Area is some 6 miles below the crossing and is reached by taking Forest Service Road 303 off SH 63. A Forest Service road also provides access to the river near the mouth of Boykin Creek about 10 miles below the SH 69 crossing. This road is reached via SH 63, Forest Service Road 313 to the Boykin Springs Recreation Area and then Forest Service Road 326. FM 255 crosses between these two points, the final crossing above B. A. Steinhagen Reservoir. A TPWL boat ramp is below the crossing.

The section from B. A. Steinhagen Lake at Town Bluff Dam all the way to US 96 near Evadale is 54 miles of popular waterway flowing through much of what is known as the "Big Thicket." The stream is 150 to 200 feet wide, making the downed trees not so much of a problem. Cypress swamps intermixed with the pine and hardwoods are plentiful.

In heavily wooded areas, watch for "strainers." These dangerous obstructions, such as brush, fallen trees, or bridge pilings, allow the water to flow through but can pin a boat and occupants.

Bankfishing on the Neches River near Steinhagen remains a favorite way to spend an afternoon.

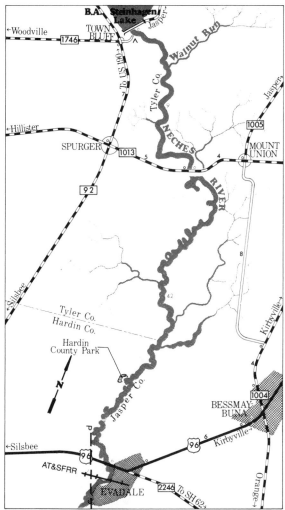

NECHES RIVER
B. A. Steinhagen Lake to US 96
54 Miles

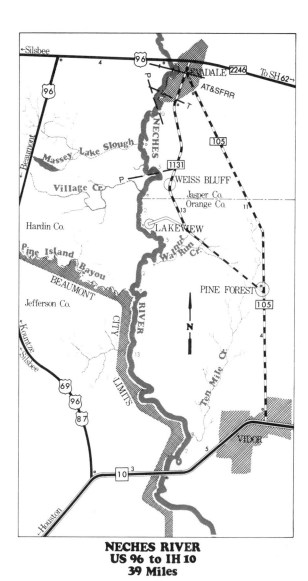

NECHES RIVER
US 96 to IH 10
39 Miles

The first crossing, FM 1013, is 12 miles below the dam with a TPWD boat ramp located here. The next crossing is a long 42 miles to US 96 about 1 mile west of Evadale and another boat ramp. Although not a crossing, the Hardin County Park is located some 10 miles back upriver where camping facilities and a TPWD boat ramp are available. The park is reached on the Camp Craven road off SH 92 northeast of Silsbee.

The final section of the Neches runs from US 96 for 39 miles to IH 10 some 5 miles west of Vidor. The river is now deep and wide with no problems for the recreational user. There are no crossings between these two highways, but there is a boat ramp in the Lakeview development about 17 river-miles below US 96. Village Creek, which will be covered later in this book, joins the Neches about 15 miles below the US 96 crossing. Nine miles below the junction of Village Creek, Pine Island

Bayou, also covered later, unites with the Neches to put a lot of fine recreational water here in this extreme southeastern part of the state.

Access to the river is very difficult at the IH 10 crossing at the eastern city limits of Beaumont. The river becomes extremely wide and is open to ocean-going vessels. Recreational boaters need to be cautious when in the vicinity of these much larger craft.

Without a doubt, the Neches River is a very important one in the eyes of the water-oriented recreationist. It offers a wealth of fishing, boating, camping, and in season, hunting. Much of the lower portion lies within the original "Big Thicket" where legends abound. By looking and listening carefully, especially late at night at your campsite, you may see or hear something that will assure that these legends will live on in you, too!

Nueces River

The two forks of the Nueces River begin in Edwards County on both sides of Rocksprings and unite just northwest of Uvalde on the way to Nueces Bay, Corpus Christi Bay, and the Gulf, a total distance of 315 miles. It is a beautiful spring-fed stream flowing through scenic canyons until it emerges from the Balcones Escarpment onto the coastal plain in northern Uvalde County. From here it flows on through semi-arid ranching country.

The name Nueces means "nuts" in Spanish, and was given to the river in 1689 by Alonso de Leon. Much earlier Cabeza de Vaca had referred to a Rio de las Nueces in this region, likely the same stream. Its original Indian name seems to have been Chotilapacquen. While crossing Texas in 1691, Teran de los Rios named the river San Diego.

The Nueces River was the early boundary line between the Spanish provinces of Texas and Nuevo Santander. After the Revolution of 1836 both Texas and Mexico claimed the territory between the Nueces and the Rio Grande. This dispute was settled by the Treaty of Guadalupe Hidalgo in 1848 which fixed the international boundary at the Rio Grande.

The river has one large impoundment, Lake Corpus Christi, located in Live Oak County between the towns of George West and Mathis. Its two main tributaries, the Atascosa River and the Frio River, join just above the town of Three Rivers and their combined flow unites with the Nueces a short distance south of town.

The only portion of the Nueces River that we will take a close look at is the 45-mile stretch of the East Prong in Real, Edwards, and Uvalde Counties from the crossing of FM 335 down to the SH 55 crossing. Like so many of the rivers in this part of the state, recreational use is difficult or restricted during normal or low water levels. During a rise or high water periods, numerous rapids do exist, some of which can be hazardous. Several spring-

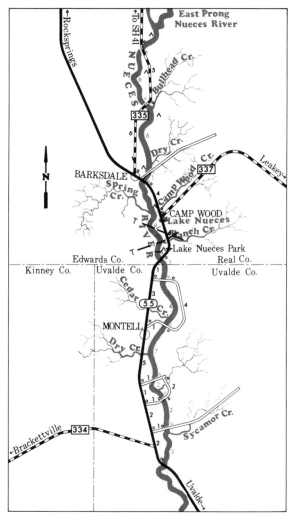

NUECES RIVER
FM 335 to SH 55
45 Miles

fed creeks enter the main stream along this stretch which help to maintain a steady, although somewhat shallow, flow. It is a very picturesque river as it flows with many twists and turns through the limestone bluffs and the small canyons of the Edwards Plateau.

As a starting point, there is a private camp located just below the junction of Hackberry Creek and the East Prong of the Nueces River some 18 miles north of Camp Wood off FM 335. Camping facilities are available here. At the FM 335 crossing 2 miles downstream, the river is shallow and wide, but deep pools can be seen above and below the crossing. Another private camp is 2 miles downriver where approximately a mile of shoreline and camping facilities are available.

Four miles downstream, FM 335 crosses the river again some 10 miles north of Camp Wood. Another private camp is located one mile below the crossing, and camping facilities are available. There is a crossing that is actually a ford off SH 55 one mile east of Barksdale where the river becomes wide and shallow. SH 55 crosses a mile farther down and good access is available here on the highway right-of-way. The next private camp is 3 miles down off SH 55 just north of Camp Wood. Camping facilities are available.

Nueces Lake Park is located 4 miles south of Camp Wood with concession stand and camping facilities. SH 55 again crosses the river a mile below the park. Good access is available here on the right-of-way. In the next 18 miles, there are five county road crossings off SH 55. Then the highway itself again crosses the river some 15 miles north-west of Uvalde.

It is in this vicinity that the Nueces flows out of the Balcones Escarpment to meander through the semi-arid ranchlands of several south Texas counties. Again, the river is shallow and not suited for recreational use except during high water periods. Good fishing is found in the area above Lake Corpus Christi and in the lake itself. This is a very busy recreational area even though it is only a few miles from the busy Gulf Coast.

Always beach your boat and plan your route before attempting to run any hazardous water.

River running is a sport that is open to anyone with a love of nature and adventure. One is not limited by age, sex, or handicap.

Paluxy River

This tributary of the mighty Brazos is only about 38 miles long from its point of origin in northeast Erath County down through Wood and Somervell counties to its junction with the Brazos, but it is a very scenic waterway with clean, clear water flowing over sand and rocks through cedar-covered hills and limestone bluffs. The two forks of the stream come together just above the community of Bluff Dale, and the 34-mile section of the river from here to the City Park in Glen Rose has definite potential for recreation during periods of adequate rainfall.

Perhaps its outstanding feature is the famous Dinosaur Valley where well-exposed dinosaur tracks have been found in the riverbed. The Dinosaur Valley State Park is located here, and camping facilities are available in the 1,204-acre park. The river at this point is a small, narrow waterway, but during periods of heavy rainfall, the river reportedly contains numerous rapids. In some places, the riverbed is composed entirely of limestone. The many sandbars along with the facilities at the Park offer plenty of places for camping and day use along the way. There are numerous road crossings, but access to the river may not be all that simple since some of these crossings are fenced.

US 377 crosses the Paluxy River in Bluff Dale, and the next crossing is a county road off FM 2870 some 8 miles downstream. Four miles farther gets you to another county road crossing off FM 204. FM 204 crosses the river in the town of Paluxy about 13 miles southwest of Granbury, but at last report, the access here is fenced off. A county road off FM 205 crosses 10 miles downstream from Paluxy at a point about one mile above the Dinosaur Valley State Park. The park is about 3 miles north-

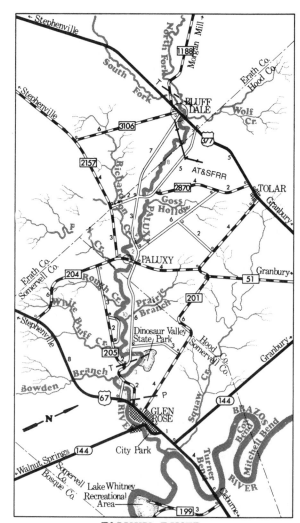

PALUXY RIVER
Bluff Dale to Glen Rose City Park
34 Miles

west of Glen Rose. FM 205 crosses 3 miles below the Park. A county road between US 67 and FM 205 crosses one mile downriver with US 67 crossing another 2 miles down, but again, access is fenced off at this point. SH 144 crosses 3 miles downstream with the Glen Rose City Park located immediately below the highway. Approximately 2 miles downstream, the Paluxy River flows into the Brazos.

For information on the Dinosaur Valley State Park and possibly the flow of the river through the area, call the park at 817/897-4588.

Pecos River

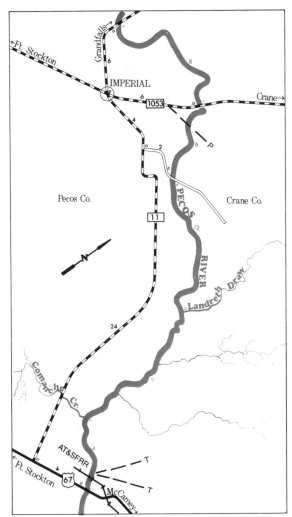

**PECOS RIVER
FM 11 to US 67 & 385
39 Miles**

A fellow by the name of Roy Bean who became the self-styled judge of the law west of the Pecos no doubt helped to spread the fame of this river as did Pecos Bill, the legendary cowboy credited with feats that some of us Texans count as commonplace. One of Zane Grey's characters who carried the name of Pecos Smith was no slouch when it came to cowboy feats of daring. And when it comes to rivers, especially in the western part of Texas, the Pecos is no "slouch!"

With its headwaters in southeastern New Mexico, it enters Texas through Red Bluff Lake and flows southeastward as the boundary between Reeves and Loving counties.

The 175-mile stretch of the river from below the Red Bluff Dam to the crossing of FM 11 west of Imperial in Pecos County has a minimal flow of water which is usually too little for recreational use. Until the river reaches the vicinity of the town of Pecos, the normal level is quite low except for periods of heavy rainfall. Its course is through the arid region of West Texas.

The 39-mile section from the FM 11 crossing down to the crossing of US 67/385 between Girvin and McCamey continues to flow through semi-arid ranching country, and the flow is still minimal. The water quality is also rather low in this area. With little or no development along its banks, the narrow width of the stream and the low water levels do not always provide conditions suitable for recreational use. During periods of adequate rainfall, some use is possible, but flash floods can be a hazard and should be expected.

Eight miles downstream from the FM 11 crossing, FM 1053 crosses at a point 6 miles northeast of Imperial. A county road crosses 6 miles downstream about 2 miles off FM 11, the last crossing before US 67/385 another 25 miles downriver.

The next 30-mile stretch of the Pecos is very similar as it remains a narrow and shallow stream flowing through the semi-arid to arid sections of

the borders of Pecos, Crane, and Crockett counties. Only during periods of rainy weather does it have enough water for recreational use, but you should remember that this is the time when flash floods are a potential hazard. The river reaches from the crossing of US 67/385 to the US 190 crossing east of Iraan. The area is relatively flat, but during the rainy periods, there can be areas of fast water. The first road crossing is that of FM 1901, some 10 miles downriver; the next is 7 miles at the crossing of FM 305. Six more miles will get you to the SH 349 crossing 6 miles north of Iraan. Then it's 7 more miles to the crossing of US 190.

As we move into the 33-mile section of the Pecos between the US 190 crossing and that of US 290, the country becomes a bit more rugged with numerous side canyons and creeks joining with the river. Still, the water is relatively shallow during most periods of the year, but during the rainy periods, the water level is excellent for recreational use. Just don't forget about the possibility of flash floods! There are some good rapids along this section, particularly in the areas of side canyons where large boulders have been tumbled into the channel. Don't let the long, quiet pools between these rapids fool you into complacency; check them out if in doubt!

SH 349 more or less parallels the river from Iraan down to Sheffield with at least three county road crossings that divide the section into convenient segments for recreational use. These are at 3 miles, another 7 miles, and the other at 9 miles with another 14 miles to the US 290 crossing. For some reason, a short portion of Interstate Highway 10 has not yet been built through here according to the latest maps. Fort Lancaster State Park, which is

for day use only due to the lack of development, is located just north of US 290 about a mile east of this crossing.

Our next division of the Pecos is a 64-mile section from the US 290 crossing down to a point known as the Pandale Crossing located 4 or 5 miles south of the Pandale Community. This is a gravel road extension from FM 2083 from near the Crockett-Val Verde County line that continues on southward to the town of Langtry on US 90 near the Rio Grande. Located in Pecos, Terrell, Crockett, and Val Verde counties, the surrounding country is very rugged with no development other than some ranching activity. During normal periods, the first half of this section is rather shallow, but below the junction with Independence Creek there is usually adequate water for recreational use. There are a lot of rapids along this portion of the

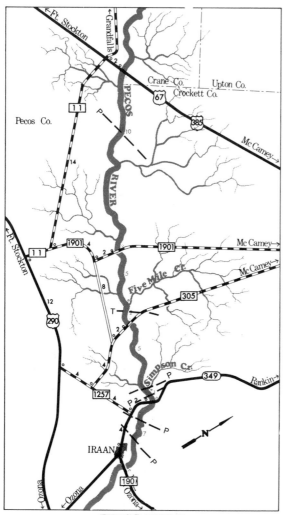

PECOS RIVER
US 67 & 385 to FM 1980
30 Miles

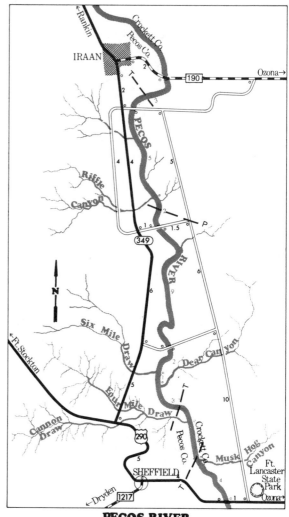

PECOS RIVER
US 190 to US 290
33 Miles

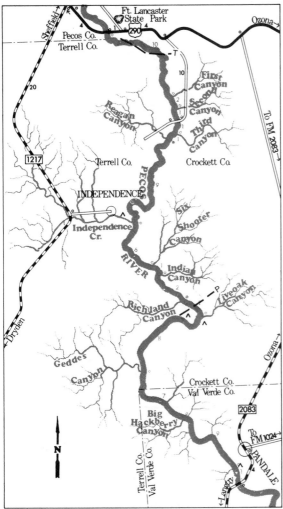

**PECOS RIVER
US 290 to Pandale Crossing
64 Miles**

If you're looking for a float trip that will take you through beautiful country that is very primitive and remote and that will test both your skill and endurance, this next 55-mile section down to the US 90 crossing between Comstock and Langtry could be the one for you. There are no in-between road crossings; just plenty of rapids and a network of canyons with walls becoming higher and higher as you travel downstream, eventually becoming several hundred feet above the river in the vicinity of the high bridge of US 90. Most of the year there is sufficient flow for recreational use; during and shortly after the rainy season, it is excellent! However, if it appears that the rainfall might be heavy even far to the north, be on the lookout for flash floods as they do occur frequently along this section.

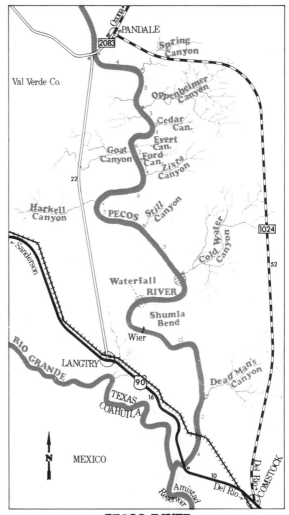

**PECOS RIVER
Pandale Crossing to US 90
55 Miles**

Pecos, again mostly near the points where the side canyons join. During the periods of heavy rainfall, flash floods can be a real hazard.

The first road crossing is a county road off US 290 about 13 miles downstream. It is approximately 11 miles on down to where Independence Creek flows into the Pecos. There is a private camp and guest ranch located at the mouth of the creek, and access to the river is available for a fee. Camping facilities are also available. A county road also comes in to the river in the Richland Canyon area another 9 miles downriver with a private camp in the vicinity. Another private camp is located on the other side of the river a couple of miles down near the junction with Liveoak Canyon. There is still another private camp located on the left a mile or two before the Pandale crossing.

The only sign that this river is bounded by desert is the fringe of cactus topping the canyon wall.

Your last chance for a takeout before getting into the big lake itself is at the old US 90 crossing that goes down to the river. There is a service station on the left going towards Langtry where, for a fee, you can get permission to leave your vehicle and a key to unlock the gate at the old highway crossing. The National Park Service reportedly has a boat ramp below the high bridge that was necessary after the construction of Amistad Dam.

While there are no public or private camping areas along this section of the Pecos, a bank of sorts has been formed along the river below the cliffs. In addition to the campsites offered along these banks, you may locate some caves that suit you better.

If you are up to it, this could be a great trip!

It is a good idea to keep up with your approximate location by keeping careful check of the canyons on the map. A major rapid is located at the mouth of Cold Water Canyon, and this one especially should be scouted before attempting to run it. It is always a good practice to take the time to scout any unfamiliar water that could be a potential hazard!

About 8 miles past the Cold Water Rapids is a weir dam that will require a short portage. From this point it isn't far until the river current begins to slow down as the water begins to back up from Amistad Reservoir on the Rio Grande. A high wind blowing up the river canyon from the south could make the paddling a bit tough from here on. When you come to the high Southern Pacific Railroad bridge, you are only about 4 miles from your takeout point at the US 90 crossing. Incidentally, this railroad bridge is some 321 feet above the normal river level.

Many of the West Texas river canyons are dotted with caves for exploration during rest stops and overnights.

Pedernales River

The Pedernales River gained national fame during the administration of President Lyndon B. Johnson due to the fact that it flows through his LBJ Ranch near Stonewall. It was well-known that one of his favorite spots was along the banks of the Pedernales!

It is a typical Hill Country stream, flowing through some rocky, rugged country for approximately 106 miles from its beginning in Kimble County to its union with the Colorado River where it becomes a part of the backwater of Lake Travis. It is a spring-fed, free-flowing river with many outstanding scenic qualities, but like so many of the other rivers of this part of the state, the flow is normally too low for recreational use. However, during periods of heavy runoff, some parts of the upper Pedernales do have exciting white water stretches. These high water conditions can be very dangerous for the inexperienced recreationist as can high water on any rocky stream. The 66-mile section from near Harper down to the US 281 crossing is extremely narrow and shallow. In addition to several county road crossings in the vicinity of Fredericksburg, the river is crossed by SH 16, US 87, US 290, and FM 1320.

Along the 39-mile section from the US 281 crossing one mile northeast of Johnson City down to the SH 71 crossing where the backwaters of Lake Travis mask the junction with the Colorado, the Pedernales is an isolated waterway flowing through some rugged country. Recreational use is feasible only during a period of rise in the flow. There are only three crossings, one at each end and the other about 7 miles from the lower end. The only other public access point is at the Pedernales Falls State Park which is about halfway between the two upper crossings. The river varies in width from 30 to 60 feet and is relatively shallow with a rise of from 1 to 2 feet affording the best float.

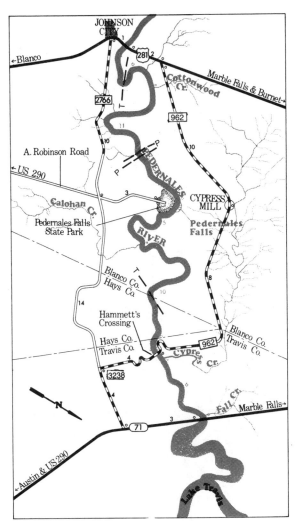

PEDERNALES RIVER
US 281 to SH 71
39 Miles

Due to the problems of portaging around Pedernales Falls, probably the best section for recreational use is the 22 miles from the park down to SH 71. There are fine facilities for camping, picnicking, swimming, and fishing at the park, but access to the river itself is a bit tough. There are two launch points here; one below the last fall, the other next to the picnic area. Both of them require the portage of all gear for 150 to 200 yards down a steep hill to the river.

There are quite a few exciting rapids on the Pedernales depending on the amount of "rise," but perhaps the only one that should be considered as dangerous is about a half mile above Hammett's

Crossing. This one is particularly hazardous if the water is high. Hammett's Crossing is on FM 962 some 25 miles west of Austin. It is a low-water crossing and affords an easy takeout for those wishing to end their float here rather than continue on the 7 miles to the SH 71 crossing. The bridge here is a high one, and takeout can be a problem. There is a private fishing camp just below the highway where parking and a much better takeout is available for a small charge.

You may wish to keep in mind that this lower portion of the Pedernales River is considered a "hot spot" for white bass during the spring run as they move up and out of Lake Travis.

As stated earlier, this is an isolated river with many natural sand and gravel bars that lend themselves to day use and camping, but because of the destructive and slovenly habits of some, the land owners tend to take a dim view of all waterway users. Don't trespass!

This kayaker navigates a chute—a narrow swift channel between obstructions that has a faster, steeper, and stronger current than the surrounding water.

A "rock garden" is a rapid that has many exposed rocks and irregular channels.

Pine Island Bayou

While not a major waterway in the sense that the larger rivers fall into that category, the bayou is included because of its potential for becoming an extremely popular stream due to its nearness to the units of the Big Thicket National Preserve. From the crossing of FM 770 about 2 miles southwest of Saratoga to the SH 326 crossing some 21 miles downstream, it flows through the Lance Rosier Unit. From that point, it becomes the Little Pine Island Bayou Corridor Unit all the way to the intersection with US 96-69-287 north of Beaumont. From there it forms the southern boundary of the Beaumont Unit to the junction with the Neches River another 8 miles downstream.

The bayou is an extremely scenic waterway as it flows through the cypress swamps and pine and hardwood bottomlands. Since it is narrow in places, brush and log jams can be a problem. During periods of high water, it is sometimes hard to

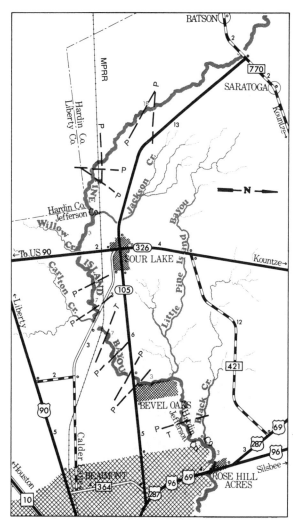

PINE ISLAND BAYOU
FM 770 To US 96, 287, & 69
49 Miles

A cypress archway makes this bayou especially scenic by canoe.

identify the main channel while floating the bayou. Since this is a part of the National Preserve, very little development is along the shoreline even when it flows through the more populated countryside.

From the crossing of FM 770 southwest of Saratoga, the location of the Big Thicket Museum, it is approximately 21 miles to the next access at the SH 326 crossing. A county road that extends off Calder Lane in Beaumont crosses the bayou another 7.5 miles downstream. From here it is another 7 miles to the SH 105 crossing 6 miles east of Sour Lake, where the road slopes gently to the bayou. Another 10 miles will get you to the US 96-69-287 crossing where a boat ramp is available. This point is on the northwest city limit of Beaumont.

An extended float could begin here through this 8-mile stretch of the bayou and on into the Neches River.

Red River

The big "Red" flows from west to east along much of the northern border of the state ultimately joining the Mississippi River. Made famous by history, legend, and even music, the Red River has played a very important part in the lives of many people. From the time when it was the boundary line between Texas and the Indian Nations, cattle drovers recognized it as one of the major milestones on the long route to the railroad and trail's end. Its 1,360 miles makes it second only to the Rio Grande in length among Texas rivers. Originating in New Mexico, the Red River's tributaries travel some 200 miles across the Panhandle with the Prairie Dog Town Fork flowing through spectacular Palo Duro Canyon. After becoming the common boundary with Oklahoma, the Salt Fork joins to form the main channel. After another 440 miles, it then separates Texas and Arkansas for 40 miles before leaving Texas to unite with the Mississippi in Louisiana.

The river takes its name from the color of the current, so pronounced that every early explorer, regardless of his language, called it "Red"; Rio Rojo or Rio Roxo in Spanish, Riviere Rouge in French, or Red River in English.

Even though the river was dangerous and sometimes a real menace to the early traveler because of its variable current and quicksand bottom, several important gateways developed along its length. One of the more famous of these is Doan's Crossing in Wilbarger County, named as the exit point for many of the north-bound cattle drives.

Lake Texoma, the largest water conservation project on the river, plays a big role in the recreational use of the river. Even though the river is the state boundary, the river itself is considered to belong wholly to Oklahoma. An Oklahoma fishing license is required, or for the lake itself, a special Lake Texoma license is available.

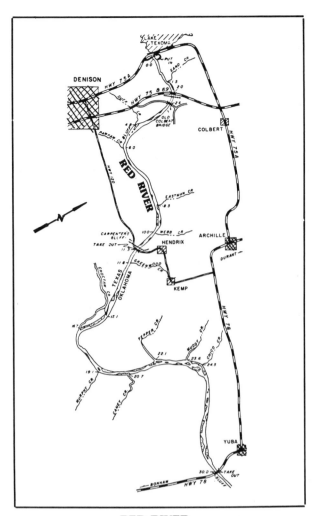

RED RIVER
Lake Texoma Dam to Hwy 78
30.0 Miles

Recreational use of the river above Lake Texoma is seasonal depending on water flow. However, below the junction with the Wichita River northeast of Wichita Falls, year-round activities are usually possible, but be very careful of quicksand. Three access points are reported for this section: the crossings of SH 79, US 81, and IH 35.

The most popular section of the river lies just below the lake and Denison Dam, especially when the dam is generating. Fortunately during the summer months, this is on the weekends. If the crest of the water release is caught, there is good floating all the way to the Arkansas line. There are access points at the highway crossings as the river flows through rather remote and rugged country. The first 30-mile section from the dam to the Highway 78 crossing makes an ideal weekend float trip,

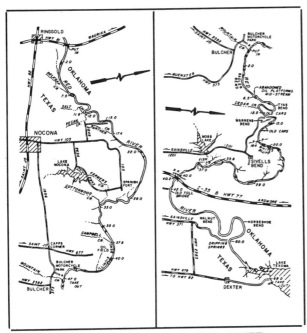

RED RIVER
Hwy 81 to Bulcher
47.0 Miles

RED RIVER
Bulcher to Lake Texana
68.0 Miles

but there is a takeout at Carpenter's Bluff after an 11-mile float. Limited camping areas are available at these points, but if you choose to camp on the bars, be sure that you're above the high water generating level. And don't forget about the quicksand!

One of Texas' rarest and most unusual fish, the paddlefish or spoonbill as it's sometimes called, is found in the river, and it is illegal to possess them. They cannot be caught using lures or bait since they live solely on zooplankton they strain from the water. Some are still caught by "snagging," a fishing method that is also illegal in Texas. The fish resemble sharks except for their broad, flat snouts which are about half their total body length.

Probably the greatest recreational offering of it all lies in the fishing for striped bass in the tailrace waters of the dam during periods of generation. When the stripers really "turn on," outdoor writer John Clift has described it as "carnival time" for the stout-hearted floodgate fishermen. For many, the river fishing is much better than that found in the lake itself. It can be kind of rugged, but the results are more than worth it!

A motorized flat-bottomed boat can make a favorite fishing spot more accessible and comfortable for the fisherman.

Rio Grande

With headwaters up in the state of Colorado, the Rio Grande flows southward through New Mexico to become the international boundary between Mexico and the State of Texas. It has a total length of nearly 1,900 miles with 1,248 of these forming the southern boundary of Texas. Due to the remoteness of the lands through which it flows, it is possibly the only river in Texas that may some day be included in the National Wild and Scenic Rivers System.

The Pueblo Indians called this river "Posoge," river of great water. "Rio de las Palmas" was the first Spanish name for it, given by Alonso Alvarez de Pineda in 1519 because of the palms his expedition found growing at its mouth. Another Mexican in 1582 followed the Rio Conchos to the point where it joined a great river which he named "Rio del Norte," River of the North. The name, Rio Grande, was first given the stream by the explorer Juan de Onate in 1598 when he discovered it at a point near present day El Paso. These names were sometimes combined into Rio Grande del Norte. Another name which many Mexicans living in the river valley sometimes still use is Rio Bravo. Several other lesser known names have been given the river by some of the early mapmakers.

One thing I'd like to make clear is that the name "Rio Grande River" is redundant. "Rio" means "river" so you would essentially be saying "River Grand River;" it is just "Rio Grande." And surely a "grand" river it is.

From its source to its mouth, the river drops 12,000 feet to sea level, changing from a snow-fed mountain stream to a desert river and finally a meandering coastal waterway. Depending on the method of measurement, the Rio Grande is either the fourth or fifth longest North American river. It is the second longest in the United States (the Missouri-Mississippi is the longest) and the longest in Texas.

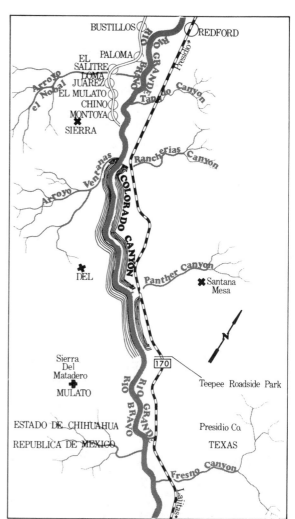

RIO GRANDE
Colorado Canyon

Due to the extensive use of river water for irrigation in New Mexico and near El Paso, the flow of the river is practically exhausted by the time it reaches the lower end of the El Paso irrigated valley. It starts up as a year-round stream again where the Rio Conchos of Mexico flows into it at Presidio-Ojinaga. As it passes on through the Big Bend area, it flows through four major canyons, the Colorado, Santa Elena, Mariscal, and Boquillas, where sometimes the canyon rim is over 1,500 feet above the river. The river flows around the base of the Chisos Mountains, and for about 100 miles forms the southern boundary of the Big Bend National Park.

Below the Big Bend, the Rio Grande gradually emerges from mountains onto the Coastal Plains, with two major reservoirs, Amistad and Falcon, both joint ventures between the United States and

Mexico. (For more information on these two big lakes, consult *A Guide to Fishing in Texas*, Lone Star Books, Houston, Texas.) Finally, the Rio Grande forms a very fertile delta where it joins the Gulf of Mexico. This is known as the Lower Rio Grande Valley, a major fruit and vegetable growing area.

There are two main rivers flowing into the Rio Grande from the Texas side, the Pecos and the Devil's River, while there are three on the Mexican side, the Rio Conchos, the Rio Salado, and the Rio San Juan. It is interesting to note that roughly three-fourths of the water running into the Rio Grande below El Paso comes from the Mexican side.

As stated earlier, the first 250-odd miles below El Paso do not contain enough water for recreational use due to the extensive use of the river water for irrigation purposes. The first section that we will consider is the 50 miles from Presidio down to Lajitas, all within Presidio County and containing Colorado Canyon. Fortunately, FM 170, El Camino del Rio, or the river road, closely parallels this portion all the way. Due to the inflow from the Rio Conchos, there is always sufficient water here for recreational use. Since it can get very hot in this part of the country in the summer, especially deep in the canyons at river level, the suggested times for floating the Rio Grande are between the latter part of October through the early part of March. Also, during the spring and fall months, the danger of flash flooding is greater.

Since I've started giving advice, I'll go a bit further and say that the Rio Grande from here all the way to Lake Amistad is *not* the place to learn canoeing or rafting or kayaking! It is isolated country and the rapids can at times be all that an experienced person can handle. If you are new at the game and feel that you've just got to do it, make sure that you go with someone who knows what he is doing. Not only that, make sure he knows that you *don't* know so that he will be able to instruct you and won't be expecting you to know how to handle each situation. I have paddled a canoe many miles on a lot of rivers, but I would not want to take a beginner as my bow-man on the Rio Grande!

To that I'll just add that even for the experienced boatman, and all the more so if that experience has been gained elsewhere, be careful! By all means, no matter who you are, check with the National Park Service in Big Bend National Park (915/477-2251) and get the river flow at the gauge station. I'd prefer 1.8 or over for canoeing on up to around 4.0. Anything over that can get mighty rough, es-

Well-engineered kayaks are practically indestructible. They don't warp, rot, leak, or require maintenance, making them a popular craft for whitewater or pleasure paddling.

pecially for canoes. Even for kayaks and large size rafts, only the experienced should make the run when the flow is between 4.5 and 7.0. When the flow exceeds this amount, such things as the fresh water springs and shoreline campsites are covered.

To make the run through Colorado Canyon, it is possible to put in a mile or two above the canyon as the river road, FM 170, runs close to the river. There are several points along here where you can drive almost up to the river. The canyon itself is about 8 miles long with a series of large rapids, said to be some of the best on the Rio Grande. The canyon is formed as the river flows around Colorado Mountain.

The first takeout point below the canyon is at the TeePee Roadside Park. The shelters here look like teepees and can be seen for a mile or so upriver as you come down. If you prefer a longer trip than this 11-mile run, the next takeout doubles the distance down to Lajitas at the edge of Brewster County and just outside the western boundary of Big Bend National Park. A road behind the trading post leads down to a slough of the river that usually contains enough water to provide access to the river itself.

Depending on the height of the flow, the rapids in this section are mostly Class II, but they can quickly become Class III or better as the water rises. As I have stated over and over again, if you're not sure of the best route to take, get out and scout the rapid before you get into it! After you've committed yourself and started through, it's too late to change your mind or your route! Especially, be on the lookout for the rapid near the mouth of Fresno Canyon. The river makes an almost 90-degree turn to the right followed by a left turn back towards the wall of the canyon. Watch out for the rocks in mid-stream.

While there are not many public campgrounds along this entire route, there are many natural campsites along the river itself. It is a good idea to set up your camp as high above the water as possible in the event of a flash flood sweeping down out of the night! Within the National Park, the Chisos Basin and Rio Grande Camp Ground are available, but it depends on the season of the year as to whether you can find space in either one. The last time I was there in late spring, they were full and running over!

The next 26-mile section of the Rio Grande includes the beautiful Santa Elena Canyon and covers that portion of the river from Lajitas down to Castolon, a small community located on the river. A float of only 17 miles will take you from Lajitas through the canyon to the first takeout at the point where Terlingua Creek joins the Rio Grande. There is a camping and picnic area here at this takeout point.

But let's go back to the put-in at Lajitas on that slough mentioned earlier. Before you commit yourself to the canyon run, take a close look at the water conditions here. If you can't see the rocks at the ford, and the water appears to be muddy and fast, I'd say wait! Unless you have plenty of time to do that waiting, perhaps it would be best to consider going elsewhere. It is likely to be mighty rough down there in the canyon itself!

It is about 12 miles from Lajitas to the entrance of Santa Elena Canyon where the river flows through a massive crack in Mesa de Anguila. The walls of the canyon tower some 1,500 feet above the river. There are several tall grassy banks that are available for day use and camping, and most of them are high enough to offer safety from any flash floods that may occur. Just inside the entrance are the Mirror Canyons, two side canyons on either side of the river that look identical.

Perhaps the most dangerous part of this float is the Rock Slide located about a quarter of a mile inside the Canyon. It was formed by the sheer wall on the Mexican side of the canyon breaking off and falling into the river. Huge rocks virtually block the river except for small channels between them. At

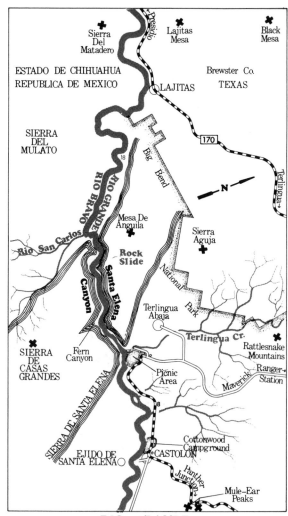

RIO GRANDE
Santa Elena Canyon

the risk of sounding overly precautious, let me insist that you do *not* try to run the Rock Slide during high water periods, and only do so during low water if you have had a lot of experience in your craft. There are some more or less "blind" areas along the way. If you feel that you must make the run, by all means beach on the Mexican side and do some serious scouting beforehand.

Fortunately, there are two alternatives to running the Slide; one is to line and portage down the Texas side if the water level is about normal. The other is for those periods of high water when a portage over the top of the slide along the Mexican side is called for. It's a rough portage, but it's better than taking any unnecessary chances. Keep in mind that once inside the canyon, you have got to go through! I would urge you never to attempt

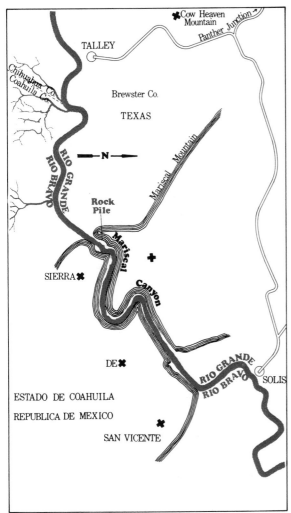

RIO GRANDE
Mariscal Canyon

desert terrain. The popularity of the major canyons greatly reduces the amount of float traffic on this section.

From Talley down to Solis is the 12-mile portion that includes Mariscal Canyon where the canyon walls rise as high as 1,800 feet and are the sheerest of any canyon on the river. A water level of about three feet is said to be the best for this trip. Since this is within the Big Bend National Park, I strongly suggest that you check with the ranger at park headquarters for the latest regulations for travel permits and camping as well as directions for following the unimproved roads to Talley and Solis. You will possibly need a campfire and boat permit, too.

Before we take a look at the canyon run itself, let me mention that it is sometimes difficult to locate the takeout point at Solis. It would be a good idea to look the surroundings over carefully at the time you leave your takeout vehicle there. Mark the takeout with something that you can spot as you come down the river. If someone is meeting you there, be sure they are where you can find them. The only visible thing around is an old shack on the Mexican side, but it is easy to miss from river level. Incidentally, this marking of takeout points is something I have said very little about so far because it usually isn't necessary. However, you be the judge, and if there is any doubt in your mind as to whether you can spot your takeout, mark it with something that you can recognize. It's a bit rough to discover a few miles downriver that you missed it!

The entrance to Mariscal Canyon, appearing as a crack in Mariscal Mountain, is about a mile and a half below Talley. Just inside the entrance is the Rockpile, a miniature of the Santa Elena Rockslide. You can easily recognize it by the huge boulder in the middle of the river. Though dangerous, it is passable with the best route being on the Texas side. You may need to be on the lookout for logs and other debris sometimes packed against it.

About a mile or less below the Rockpile is perhaps the most challenging spot on this float, the Tight Squeeze. It is so named because a huge flat-topped rock almost fills the channel. On the Texas side, there is a narrow, shallow gap that is passable if the water is low and you "walk" it through. On the right or Mexican side is a chute of white water than can be tricky even for the experienced. As it goes through this channel, the water drops three or four feet with a partially submerged rock right in the middle making it essential that the canoe or whatever make a quick left hand turn at the bottom of the chute in order to miss said rock!

floats of this kind with only one canoe or kayak, or for that matter, one raft. You could find yourself in a situation where you would need help and quick! If you do try to run the Slide, be sure to have a couple of fellows downstream with throw lines just in case. And *never* run any treacherous water without a good, personal floatation device—life-jacket, that is!

At the Santa Elena Canyon exit where Terlingua Creek enters the river, there is a National Park Service Camp Ground. Seven miles downstream is the little village of Castolon on the river with good access to the river itself.

The next 40 miles of the Rio Grande is not as spectacular as the sections with the deep canyons, but is nevertheless a fine recreational waterway that can be enjoyed by persons with less experience since the river flows through relatively flat

The good part about the "Squeeze" is that no matter what the water level might be, there is a spot to take out about 50 yards above for a chance to have a look-see before entering. Take your time and really study the river conditions as they are at the time. Any time that I'm in doubt, I take the safest route!

The rest of the canyon is beautiful with no more real challenges. A couple of miles below the Squeeze the canyon walls draw back from the river for about a quarter of a mile. On the Mexican side, near the point where a dry creek enters, there are some Indian petroglyphs etched on a boulder. An old Indian trail and some old dugouts that are sometimes inhabited by Mexicans might be of interest to some. It is about 25 miles from the Mariscal Canyon exit through open desert country to the takeout at Solis.

The next section of the Rio Grande covers about 19.5 miles from Solis down to the ford that crosses to Boquillas, Mexico. This is also the location of the Rio Grande Village, the campground operated by the National Park Service. Two relatively short canyons are located in this section, San Vicente and Hot Springs Canyons. There is sufficient water here almost all the time for recreational use and the possible hazards are few.

You can begin your trip through this next 19.5 mile section at Solis as already described, or you might want to continue your trip through Mariscal Canyon. This would mean a longer float, of course, but it would eliminate the trouble of getting into and then finding the takeout at Solis. San Vicente Canyon, with walls rising several hundred feet above the river, begins about a mile downstream from Solis and continues for about 3 miles.

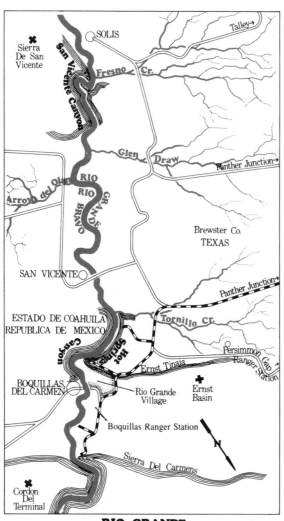

RIO GRANDE
San Vicente &
Hot Springs Canyons

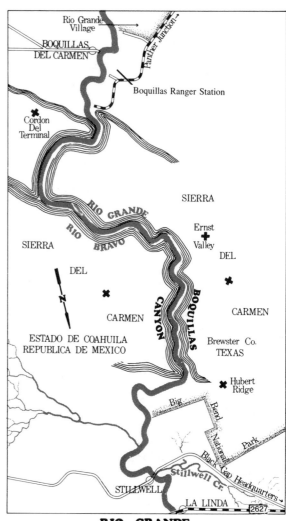

RIO GRANDE
Boquillas Canyon

About a mile below the canyon exit, Glen Draw enters from the Texas side with a rapid at the mouth of the creek. Tornillo Creek next joins the river on the Texas side another 11 miles downstream. Although there is usually only a small flow of water from the creek, there is a rapid at the junction. Several hot springs are located in the vicinity of the creek. There was once a vacation resort located here because of these springs.

The Hot Springs Canyon entrance is about a half mile downriver, and there are numerous hot springs within the 2-mile length of the canyon. At the canyon exit, the river flows from what is called the Ernst Tinaja. From here it is only another mile to the ford and the Rio Grande Village. The ford is a good point of access to the river.

A reminder once again that a National Park Service campfire/boat permit is required before any recreational use of the river is allowed. This also applies to this next section through Boquillas Canyon since it, too, lies within the boundaries of the Big Bend National Park.

This 26-mile portion that includes Boquillas Canyon is very scenic with no potentially hazardous places and usually plenty of water for recreational use. However, it does not get the traffic of the upstream canyons due to the restricted access. The access at the lower end is at the Stillwell Crossing on the U. J. Adams Ranch, and permission must be obtained either from the owner in Alpine or at the ranch. There is a per-person charge by the ranch, and also a charge for leaving a vehicle there. It's worth it though, since said vehicle will be safe and there when you get back.

Another access point is the La Linda Crossing on FM 2627 that runs through the Black Gap Management Area. There is a toll bridge here and a U.S. Border Port of Entry.

There is still another access point at a road that goes through the Black Gap Wildlife Management Area that is not shown on the accompanying map nor is it shown on the Brewster County Highway Map. It runs down to the point where the Maravillas Canyon, the fourth Texas-side canyon past the La Linda crossing, joins the main stream. I would definitely check at Black Gap (915/376-2216) before making this run or using the road. When you get there, check in with the headquarters office.

The next portion of the Rio Grande just might be the toughest of them all since it is over 90 miles from the Stillwell Crossing and just a bit shorter from the La Linda bridge down to the takeout at the Dudley Harrison Ranch some 20 miles south of Dryden. There is said to be a Texaco sign on the bank of the river and a gauging station about a quarter of a mile above the takeout point. For more information and permission, call Mr. Harrison in Sanderson at 915/345-2503 or at his home at 915/345-2403. There is a per-person charge and a fee for leaving your vehicle at the ranch, but it's worth it!

If you want to make the entire trip through the lower canyons and go all the way to Langtry, the trip covers about 135 miles. Using the Maravillas Creek road as a put-in will shorten the run by about 12 miles. Before you even consider making this trip, either the 90-mile one or the full distance, take a close look at yourself and the other members of your party. Even the 90-mile trip will take al-

One of the safest ways for a novice to experience whitewater is to join one of the many organized river rafting tours through the Rio Grande.

most a week, the full one another three or four days. That's a long time to be on the river, so each participant should be in good physical condition. Your equipment should be first-rate and your supplies should be adequate and well-protected. You're going to have to do quite a bit of portaging around some of the tough rapids along the way.

Now, let's go back and take a closer look just in case you decide to try it. These are just some of the things you'll encounter along the way.

If you do start out at the Stillwell Crossing, you'll find a good campsite at the Maravillas Canyon, or if you wish to go a bit farther, the Outlaw Flats are only 5 miles downriver. These are simply some flat lands on both sides of the river. A couple of miles down on the Mexican side you'll see Castle Butte, sometimes called El Capitan, that rises about a thousand feet above the desert floor. Another 5 miles will take you to Big Canyon entering from the Texas side. The rapids are not too bad, and there are some warm springs in the area if you care to take a hot bath! You can also replenish your drinking water supply here.

Just a mile downstream is the Reagan Canyon that enters from the Texas side and is marked by a spectacular rise in the wall. The next 40 miles of the river canyon is also sometimes known as Reagan Canyon, Bullis Canyon, or Canyon de Lleguas. An old stone cabin may still be visible on the Texas side at the canyon entry point.

The San Rocendo Canyon is a large one that enters from the Mexican side some 12.5 miles farther down; Dagger Mountain is directly across on the Texas side. Here we find Hot Springs Rapid at the base of the canyon. This can be a rough one, and under most conditions, you should portage on the Mexican side. About 50 yards below the rapid on the same side is a hot spring. This is considered a good campsite area and a chance to again replenish drinking water supplies. About 5 miles or so farther along, there is a tricky little rapid that often gives canoeists trouble. You can recognize it by the big flat ledge on the Texas side and some big rocks in the middle of the stream. Take a look from the Texas side before you try it. There is another rapid about 3 miles down from this one, but it isn't nearly as tough.

The next one will make up for it though at the base of Burro Bluff, a high sheer bluff on the Texas side about 8 miles downstream. The Burro Bluff Rapid, also known as Upper Madison Falls, comes in two sections. While the upper section is sometimes O.K. to run, a mistake here would put you in serious trouble since the lower section, only 200 feet away, is definitely impassable. Either portage

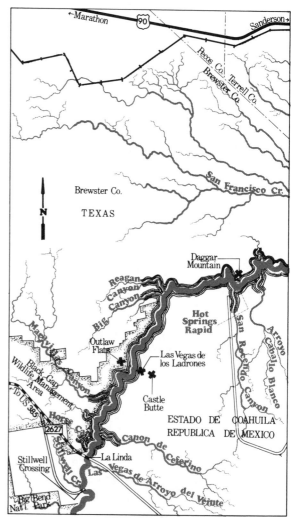

**RIO GRANDE
Lower Canyons**

around both or else line through the first section, then paddle to the Mexican side and portage. There are some good campsites in this area if it fits in with your schedule to make an overnight stay here.

The Lower Madison Falls, also known as the Horseshoe Falls, is 3 or 4 miles downstream. A horseshoe-shaped barrier has been caused here by a rockfall, and there is no safe channel, only a very dangerous rapid. You can portage on either side, but the Texas side is the better way. There are several hot springs in the vicinity of these falls. A short distance below there is a big spring that flows from beneath a big rock. This is a good place to again replenish your water supply for the final part of this long float.

Panther Canyon is next, coming in from the Texas side. There are several large caves in the canyon walls that you might like to explore. The Pan-

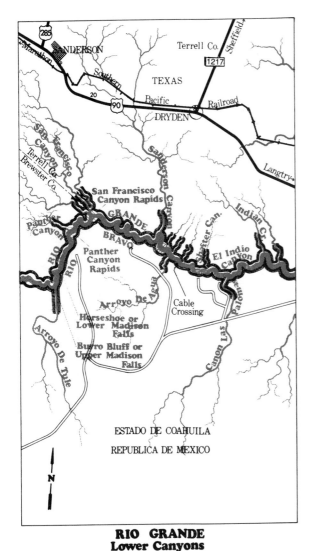

RIO GRANDE
Lower Canyons

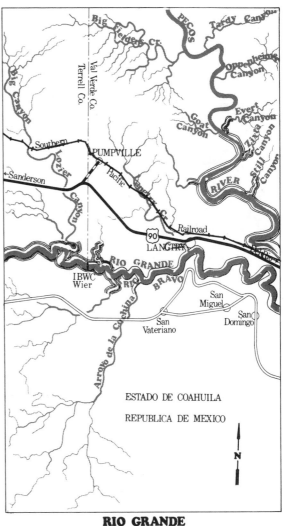

RIO GRANDE
Lower Canyons

ther Rapids are also located here, and they can be very rough at times. They can be run on the Texas side by experienced hands, but even they should be extra careful and alert. These rapids are about 2.5 miles below the Lower Madison Falls.

Another 5 or 6 miles will take you to the mouth of San Francisco Canyon, a wide canyon that enters from the Texas side. The San Francisco Canyon Rapids are here, too, and they present a real challenge even for the most experienced. The current sweeps against the canyon wall, and extreme caution should be exercised. Look them over very carefully before you make the run.

It is about 12 miles to the entry point of the next big canyon from the Texas side, Sanderson Canyon. About 2.5 miles past this point, the Sanderson Canyon Rapids offer another real challenge that should be well scouted before an attempt is made to run them. In some situations, such as

fairly high water, this one should not be run, and a portage is in order.

If you plan to take out at the Harrison Ranch mentioned earlier, it is about 5 miles past those last rapids, so be on the lookout for the Texaco sign and the gauging station. This is also known as the Dryden Crossing, and at one time there was a cable crossing at this point. There are only some old ladders and the remains of old buildings at the site now.

For those who wish to continue on to Langtry, there is a ford about 3 miles down known as Shafter Crossing that is just upstream from Shafter Canyon. At one time there was a primitive dirt road that led back to Dryden. Four miles downriver is the beginning of El Indio Canyon, a sheer canyon that is about 8 miles long. Take your time as you proceed through this last section down to Langtry so as not to be caught by surprise in

The Rio Grande is not the place to learn whitewater canoeing. It is isolated country with rapids that are sometimes all an experienced canoeist can handle.

case the river conditions are such that a particular stretch could cause a problem.

It's a long run down to the next big canyon, some 24 miles to the point where Lozier Canyon enters from the Texas side. The walls of the canyon begin to lower from here on. Five miles farther in the vicinity of the Terrell-Val Verde County Line is an International Boundary Water Commission weir dam that marks the backwaters of Amistad Reservoir. You still have about 18 miles to go to make it to Langtry where a dirt road comes down to the river. From here it is roughly 30 miles to where the Pecos River joins the Rio Grande and perhaps another 10 miles to the head of Amistad Reservoir.

There is still a lot of river from the Amistad Dam on to the Gulf of Mexico. Falcon Dam and Reservoir is located in Zapata County above Rio Grande City and below Laredo. The surrounding terrain grows decreasingly rugged as it goes toward the coast. The countryside changes from semi-arid brush lands to the semi-tropical regions of far South Texas. There is always sufficient water available for recreational use throughout this portion. However, as the water meanders slowly through here, a run of about 500 miles on its way to the Gulf, the water quality tends to deteriorate due to the number of villages, towns, and cities that are located along the river.

There is one small waterfall, Kingsbury Falls, located in Maverick County south of Eagle Pass just below El Indio. El Indio is 18 highway miles south of Eagle Pass on FM 1021. This waterfall is potentially dangerous especially if the water level is above normal. There are many isolated stretches along the lower portion of the Rio Grande, but ac-

cess points and road crossings become more frequent as the river approaches the coast. Even though the country does seem empty and isolated along much of the entire route of the Rio Grande, you should remember that all the land on the Texas side is either within the National Park, the Wildlife Management Area, or is privately owned. Use it with care, and leave it better than you found it. I like the old saying "Take nothing but pictures and leave nothing but footprints!"

The bowman has an unobstructed view as the mysteries of the Rio Grande unfold around each bend.

Sabine River

With a place of prominence in early history and with a name that comes from the Spanish word meaning "cypress," the Sabine River has its beginning in Collin and Hunt counties and flows southeast and south through hardwood bottoms and the piney woods all the way to Sabine Lake and the Gulf of Mexico. It has the largest discharge at its mouth of any river in Texas, some 6.8 million acre-feet of water annually. The lower Sabine is the eastern boundary of Texas, although for a time there was a dispute as to whether the Sabine or the Arroyo Hondo east in Louisiana was the boundary. There was also a dispute in which it was alleged that the Neches River was really the Sabine and therefore the boundary. For years the area along the Sabine was a so-called Neutral Ground and was infested with outlaws.

As with other rivers that have been dammed, the fame of the impoundments often far exceeds the river in the eyes of the outdoor recreationist. The first of two big ones, Lake Tawakoni, east of Dallas, is a water storage reservoir which largely controls the upper portion of the river. The lake itself is a fine recreational facility, but the river below it often does not have sufficient flow for much recreational use. Water is released from the dam only when the lake level exceeds the conservation pool. Too, the river here is narrow, and log jams and brush can make navigation very difficult.

Toledo Bend Reservoir, which filled to the top of the power pool at 172 feet elevation mean sea level in 1968, has received nationwide publicity as one of the hottest bass fishing lakes in the country. Because of the tremendous amount of timber and underbrush that was flooded when the lake filled, it is an ideal fishery and should continue as one for many years to come.

Back in the days of the stern-wheelers, river boats hauled timber, cotton and other freight as far upriver as Logansport. They literally put themselves out of business as they helped to haul mate-

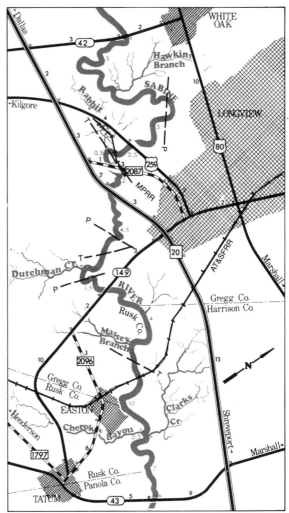

SABINE RIVER
SH 42 to SH 43
44.5 Miles

rials used in the construction of the new railroads whose cheaper freight rates brought the end of the riverboat era just before the turn of the century.

Except in those places where the river was fordable, a ferry was the usual method of crossing. One history book on the riverboat era lists 69 such ferries and landings on the Sabine. Pendleton Bridge that now spans Toledo Bend Lake is just below the site of Pendleton Ferry, once one of the major gateways to Texas.

Recreational boating on the Sabine, particularly for canoes or flat-bottomed john-boats, can begin at the SH 42 crossing 2 miles south of White Oak. There is about 200 feet of shoreline available on the highway right-of-way. The use of such areas will eliminate the danger of trespassing on private property. Throughout most of the river's length, sand bars are available for camping and day use.

Be on the lookout for log jams and drifts on this stretch of the river, too.

This 44.5-mile section from SH 42 to SH 43 between Marshall and Tatum has become more popular as a recreational area with the continuing effort to control the pollution from the cities and the industries of the area. A small 2–3-foot waterfall spans the river about 2 miles below the SH 42 crossing. Other access points on this portion include the US 259 crossing 2 miles southwest of Longview with nearly 500 feet of shoreline available on the right-of-way. FM 2087 some 3 miles southwest of Longview has about 300 feet of shoreline available. The SH 149 crossing 3 miles south of Longview has some 200 feet of shoreline on the right-of-way. At the SH 43 crossing, a boat ramp is available on the road right-of-way.

The next section is 41 miles through Harrison and Panola counties down to FM 2517 known as the Deadwood Road. This is a scenic float through forests of giant cypress, pine, and various hardwoods and can be made in larger boats except during periods of relatively low water. For floaters using either a canoe or a john-boat, there is plenty of water. Several larger creeks join the river through here adding to the flow.

There has been a lot of strip mining for lignite around Beckville and Tatum, but with the stringent controls now in effect, there should be little evidence of this in the surface runoff that finds its way into the river.

The next crossing is at US 59 about 11 miles north of Carthage with 100 yards of shoreline in the right-of-way. FM 1794 crosses about 8 miles north of Carthage with 11.5 miles of river downstream to the US 79 crossing. A TPWD boat ramp is available, but the floater should keep in mind that during periods of low water, he may have a problem using the larger boats. The next 12 miles of river down to the FM 2517 crossing is an excellent day float. There is another TPWD boat ramp here. This is the last road crossing above Toledo Bend Reservoir except for the one at Logansport where it still maintains the appearance of the river.

If the lake level is only slightly below the top of the power pool at 172-foot elevation, this section from Logansport up to FM 2517 can be made in a bass boat with its big motor. There are some beautiful sand bars along this stetch, and even though there are several private camps and ramps along the way, it isn't likely to be too crowded to offer plenty of seclusion.

Toledo Bend Reservoir extends some 65 miles from Logansport to the dam. (See *A Guide to Texas Lakes* and *A Guide to Fishing in Texas*, Lone Star

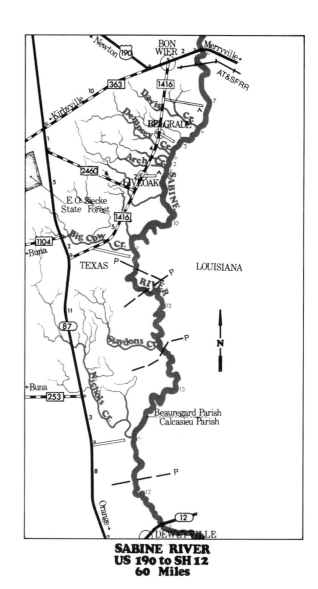

SABINE RIVER
US 190 to SH 12
60 Miles

Books, Houston Texas, as sources of information on the excellent opportunities for outdoor recreation on this huge lake.)

There are several stories as to the source of the name Toledo Bend, but this one is my favorite: Way back when the early Spanish explorers were first coming into Louisiana and Texas, a party of adventurers moving up the river was ambushed and killed by a roving band of hostile Indians. When the tragedy was later discovered by another group of explorers, they found items that had been carried by the first group and had been overlooked by the looting Indians that bore the stamp of Toledo, Spain. From then on, the spot was known as Toledo Bend, and it is in that area that the giant earthen dam forming the 181,600-acre reservoir was built.

The very remote Sabine is an all-season river with a slow-moving current and clean, white sandbars.

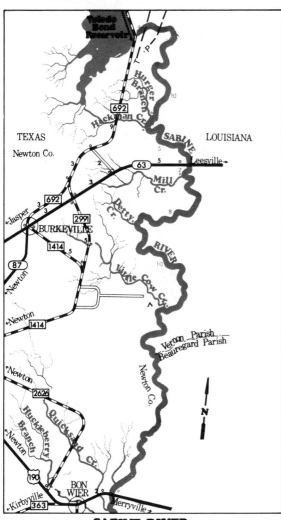

SABINE RIVER
Toledo Bend Dam to US 190
56 Miles

There is a short section just below the spillway gates that, during periods of light discharge, can be fine for the canoeist. The river has carved through the soapstone a channel that is somewhat reminiscent of the float streams of the West. The water quality here below the dam is very good.

It is approximately 150 miles from Toledo Bend Dam to the Gulf of Mexico. There is usually enough discharge from the dam to afford adequate water all the way, and the many creeks and bayous that flow into it add to the volume all the way. The river forms the boundary between Texas and Louisiana. The banks gradually take on a more swamp-like appearance as you move south.

The section from the dam to the US 190 crossing east of Bon Wier is about 56 river-miles. There is only one highway crossing in between, that of SH 63 between Burkeville and Leesville, Louisiana, although there is a dirt road off FM 1414 that goes to the mouth of Little Cow Creek (see map) to an area that is reportedly open to the public. There is a concrete launching ramp at the US 190 bridge, but the last time I was there in early fall, there was about 150 feet of sand bar between the ramp and the river!

With many sand bars for camping or day use along the way, this section is one of the more scenic, quality waterways of the state. Starting from below the dam at 75 to 100 feet wide, the river gradually widens to about 300 feet at the crossing of IH 10 at Orange. From here on, the river is deep enough for ocean-going vessels.

The section from US 190 down to the SH 12 crossing covers some 60 miles through scenic bot-

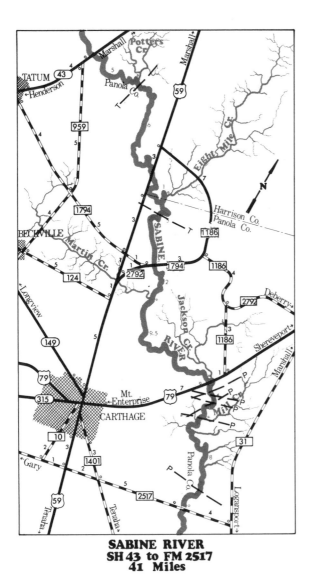

**SABINE RIVER
SH 43 to FM 2517
41 Miles**

There is a county road off SH 87 north of Deweyville that goes in to the mouth of Nichols Creek where a boat ramp of sorts is available.

River use and shoreline development increases from the SH 12 crossing on to IH 10 and the Gulf, but it is still a very scenic waterway with adequate, high quality water at all times for recreational use. With only a bit of imagination, one can almost hear the throb of the steam engines of the early sternwheelers as they wended their way northward to the many landings of days gone by. The once ever-present danger of Indian attack is no more, but the modern day explorer will still press on in his desire to "see what lies around the next bend of the river!"

The Spanish moss-draped cypress trees create a romantic backdrop for exploring the Sabine.

tomlands with big cypress and hardwoods festooned with Spanish moss. The river is deep and slow-moving and offers some large creeks that can be explored in canoes or small boats. Several county roads off FM 1416 offer some in-between points of access, but it is best to inquire locally as to the type of access and if it is open to the public.

San Antonio River

Known to millions for its development into a parkway within the city of San Antonio, the river has its origin at the large springs within and near the corporate limits of the city. No visitor to that city should fail to stroll along the waterside walkways or take a ride in either a rented paddleboat or the open-deck "taxi-boats" that travel the downtown stream with the regularity of a city bus. The visitor can enjoy a wide variety of outdoor cafes and specialty shops that line the waterway, nestled beneath the tall buildings of the city that boasts of both the "old" and the "new."

Where else can you dine on the cuisine of your choice while pigeons light on the backs of chairs and the more brave ones even hop onto the table to steal a bite of your food? A glance at the pale, blue-green water of the river could reveal a large school of fish attacking a scrap of bread thrown into the stream. They are likely to hang around, too, until disturbed by one of the paddleboats or barges or the small cruisers used by the police as they patrol the waterway.

From its spring-fed beginning in San Antonio, the river flows some 180 miles through the coastal plain until it joins with the Guadalupe River a few miles above the point where it flows into San Antonio Bay on the Gulf. Because its two main tributaries, Cibolo Creek and the Medina River, are also spring-fed, the San Antonio River has a remarkably steady flow of clear water. The average annual runoff is relatively small since its watershed is limited and somewhat arid, but because of the springs, it is one of the steadiest of Texas rivers.

It was first named the Leon by Alonso de Leon during his trip across Texas in 1689. However, he was not naming the river after himself; he called it "lion" because the channel was filled with a rampaging flood at the time.

The first 48-mile section of the river from downtown San Antonio to Floresville is available for general recreational use with numerous road

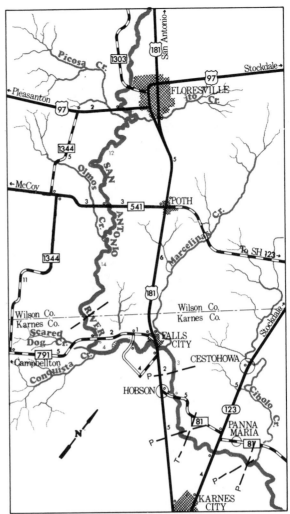

SAN ANTONIO RIVER
Floresville to Hobson
36 Miles

crossings which provide access to most sections of the river. The Medina River unites with the San Antonio just south of the city, thus adding substantially to the flow.

The portion of the river that we have mapped is the 41-mile stretch from Floresville to the SH 123 crossing 4 miles north of Karnes City. The river will run from 50 to 75 feet wide as it meanders between steep, earthen banks lined with elm, sycamore, willow, and cottonwood trees. There are no problem rapids, but there are a couple of waterfalls. Occasional log jams may slow you down as some of them will require a portage.

From the US 97 crossing one mile southwest of Floresville, it is 12 miles down to the next crossing at FM 541 6 miles south of Floresville. From here it is 14 miles on to the FM 791 crossing, 3 miles

Canoes are easily transported either singly atop your car or "en masse" on a specially built canoe trailer, such as this one.

southwest of Falls City. A waterfall known as Skiles Falls is approximately 3 miles downstream from this crossing. A county road off FM 791 one mile southwest of Falls City crosses the river about a mile below the falls. The second waterfall is located about 1.5 miles downstream from here and about one mile upstream from the crossing of US 181 near Falls City's southeastern city limits.

FM 81 crosses the river 3 miles downstream about one mile east of Hobson. The SH 123 crossing is approximately 5 river miles away. For those wishing to further explore this typical coastal river,

other road crossings include SH 80, SH 72, SH 239, US 59 southwest of Goliad, and US 77A-183. Goliad State Park, a Texas historical highlight, is located adjacent to the river in this section. US 77 crosses the river near McFaddin a few miles above the junction with the Guadalupe River.

Although the lower sections of the San Antonio River experience a reduction in water quality, the Texas Water Quality Board considers it above the minimum level for water-contact sports despite its somewhat murky look. Log jams can still be a problem along this isolated portion of the river.

A rental agent insures that with life jackets, hats for sun protection, and paddles of the appropriate length for each person these canoeists are ready for a safe and pleasant river trip.

San Bernard River

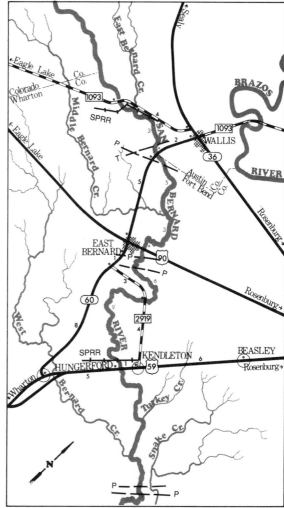

SAN BERNARD RIVER
FM 1093 to US 59
27 Miles

A small river in comparison to its neighbor to the east, the Brazos, the San Bernard is only 125 miles in length, and is best described as a coastal river located entirely in the coastal plain. The upper portions usually do not contain enough water for recreational use, and quite often, log and brush jams created by the hardwoods growing along its banks become a problem.

The main section that has potential as a recreational waterway is a 27-mile stretch from the FM 1093 crossing southwest of Wallis to the US 59 crossing between Hungerford and Rosenberg. There are several springs along the course of the river providing a minimum flow of good quality water. The channel is quite narrow and during periods of high water is ill-defined.

Four miles downstream from FM 1093 is the SH 60 crossing between East Bernard and Wallis. The next crossing is that of US 90A in the eastern city limits of East Bernard. Here again, the river is narrow and the main channel is hard to distinguish. FM 2916 crosses the river 6 miles downstream at a point between SH 60 and US 59. Another 9 miles of river gets you to the US 59 crossing near Kendleton.

The 70-mile section from US 59 on to the Gulf of Mexico is suitable for recreational use year round as it winds through coastal prairie. The banks are lined with heavy vegetation, and there are numerous springs. There is one low-water dam located between FM 1301 and SH 35 near West Columbia that can be a problem for recreational use. The river enters the Gulf about 4 miles below the entry point of the Brazos southwest of Freeport.

The current is not constant all over the river. Due to friction, which slows the water on the bottom and along the banks, the fastest flow is on the surface in midstream.

San Gabriel River

Formed at Georgetown by the union of the North and South Forks, the San Gabriel River flows some 65 miles through Williamson and Milam counties to join the Little River to the north of Rockdale. Two relatively new reservoirs are located on the river, and these have added significantly to the fishing potential for the outdoor recreationists.

Lake Georgetown is located on the North Fork of the San Gabriel some 4 miles north of Georgetown and contains some 1,310 acres that promise to be an outstanding recreational area. The lake was known in the beginning as North Fork Lake. Granger Lake with its 4,400 surface acres is located on the river southeast of Granger. The Texas Parks and Wildlife Department plans to manage Lake Georgetown mainly for smallmouth bass due to its rocky habitat. Granger Lake is more suited to largemouth bass and catfish. Original stockings of the lake included 26,000 Florida bass fry and 31,860 channel catfish fingerlings. It is also expected to develop into a good crappie fishery. It is certainly likely that the areas above and below both lakes will also become top fishing spots. The lakes were opened to fishing and boating on March 1, 1981.

The flow of the river itself will be largely dependent on the amount of water released from both these dams. Except for any unusually dry summer periods, there should be enough water for recreational use.

The section of the North Fork above Georgetown Lake, though not mapped here, is worth investigation by anyone wishing to explore a small river and get away from the crowds that are sometimes found on the larger and better-known streams. With its headwaters in Burnet County, it

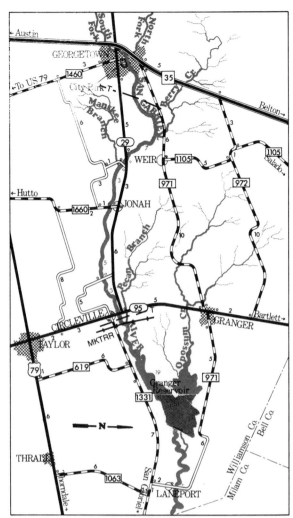

SAN GABRIEL RIVER
Georgetown City Park to Laneport
37.5 Miles

flows generally southward through Burnet County into Williamson County and into the lake. This section is a scenic, winding river through the typical limestone formations of the Edwards Plateau. Floating of the river is restricted to periods of abundant rainfall as it does not have a steady flow the year round.

First access is at a county road crossing off FM 2340 about 8 miles northeast of Burnet. FM 963 crosses the river 8 miles northeast of Burnet also. FM 243 and a county road cross the river in the vicinity of Bertram. There are three county road crossings off US 183 north of Liberty Hill, and US 183 crosses 3 miles northeast of Liberty Hill. The backwaters of Lake Georgetown begin a short distance past this crossing with the dam itself located about 3 miles upstream from the IH 35 crossing in Georgetown.

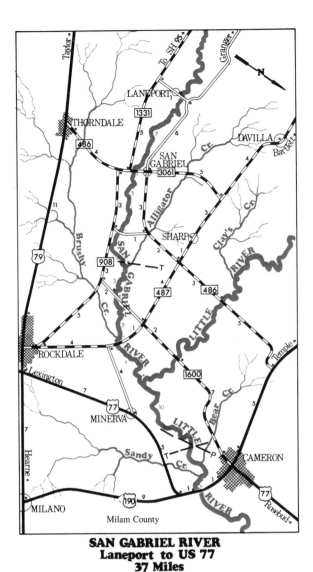

SAN GABRIEL RIVER
Laneport to US 77
37 Miles

its of Georgetown. There is a small lake at the City Park in Georgetown near the confluence of the North and South Forks of the San Gabriel River.

There are two sections of the main stream that offer recreational opportunities especially for the novice. Although there are numerous small rapids to add some spice to a float, none of them present any hazardous situations. The flow is partially dependent on the release of water from the two reservoirs, but there is generally enough minimum flow to allow use of the river.

The first portion is the 37.5-mile stretch from the Georgetown City Park to a county road crossing off FM 1331 in the town of Laneport. There is a good entry point in the park with about a half mile of shoreline for access as well as rest rooms and picnic tables. Seven miles downstream is the SH 29 crossing where about 250 feet of shoreline are available. A county road crosses another half mile downriver, with the FM 1660 crossing at Jonah some 3 miles down. The last road crossing above Granger Lake is that of SH 95 in the town of Circleville between Granger and Taylor. The lake was built and is operated by the U.S. Army Corps of Engineers with boat ramps and other facilities available for recreationists. The first road crossing below the dam is a county road off FM 1331 in the town of Laneport several miles downstream.

Another 37-mile stretch of the San Gabriel River that offers recreational opportunities most of the time reaches from the Laneport crossing on past the junction with Little River to the US 77 crossing near Cameron. This section of the river seems to have higher banks that restrict the boater's view. Depending on the height of the flow, there is an occasional small rapid or area of fast water to liven things up. Access is available at several road crossings along the way.

Seven miles below the Laneport crossing is that of FM 486. A county road then crosses another 5 miles downriver. The next crossing is 6 miles away at a county road between FM 487 and FM 908. FM 487 crosses the river 5 miles below with the junction of the San Gabriel and the Little River about 4 miles below this crossing. Recreational use can then be continued on to the crossing of US 77 one mile southeast of Cameron.

The South Fork of the San Gabriel is very similar to the North Fork and has a length of about 34 miles. It does not have a steady flow of water and recreational use is limited to periods of sufficient rainfall. It, too, is a scenic river with numerous limestone bluffs, and is worth investigation by anyone wishing to explore a small stream. It is crossed by FM 243, FM 1174, FM 1869, US 183, several county roads, and IH 35 near the west city lim-

San Jacinto River

The East and West forks join together in the northeastern part of Harris County above Houston. A dam just below the confluence of these two forks forms Lake Houston. The lower portion of the main stream forms a part of the Houston Ship Channel and flows directly into the Gulf. For this reason, the river in this section is not suitable for recreational use.

Also, the flow of water in the East Fork is usually too low for boating or canoeing. However, a dam across the West Fork in Montgomery County forms Lake Conroe, a recreational high spot near the huge metropolitan area. Except for those periods of low rainfall and during periods of no generation of power and no release of water through the dam, the portion of the West Fork from immediately below the dam down to the US 59 crossing can offer a scenic and pleasant float. Brush and log jams can sometimes present a problem, but these are to be expected along the narrow stretches of our eastern streams.

Since the dam does not have a set generating schedule or a minimum daily release, some advance checking is needed before planning a float down this 34-mile section of the West Fork. In addition to the SH 105 crossing, FM 2854 crosses some 3 miles downstream with about 400 yards of shoreline available on the highway right-of-way. The next crossing is that of IH 45 south of Conroe another 8 miles downstream. It is about 23 more miles to the US 59 crossing located on the northeastern city limits of Humble. A TPWD boat ramp is located here along with private camps on both sides of the river that have picnicking facilities available. The river flows into Lake Houston just below this crossing.

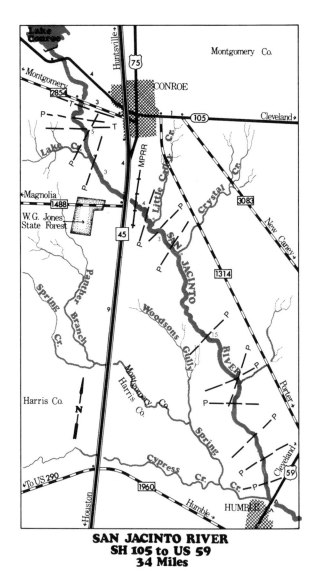

SAN JACINTO RIVER
SH 105 to US 59
34 Miles

While the river itself is not particularly noted for its recreational opportunities, both Lake Conroe and Lake Houston are important to the area. Perhaps the river's greatest claim to fame lies in the fact that the battle of San Jacinto freeing Texas from domination by Mexico was fought on its banks. There are two stories of the origin of the name: One states that when the river was first discovered by early explorers, they found the channel choked with hyacinth; the other claims that it was discovered on August 17, St. Hyacinth's Day. Take your pick!

San Marcos River

Few would argue that this is one of the most popular recreational rivers in all of Texas for canoeing and floating. Most of it is suitable for a family-type outing, especially for those with some previous experience. There are some hazards along the way, but with proper care and caution, these can be handled with no problems. Be prepared to get wet and make sure that your gear is as waterproof as possible. It is not a "big" river in terms of width and water flow, but there are few places "bigger" in the sense of being used by so many people. Its location between Austin and San Antonio makes it readily accessible to a rather large segment of the state population.

The river is formed near the north city limits of the town of San Marcos by several large springs with a flow of about 100 cubic feet per second. The spring flow is second only to Comal Springs at New Braunfels which averages 303 cubic feet per second. A very popular commercial attraction, Aquarena Springs, is located here at the head of the river. From this point, it flows approximately 75 miles to unite with the Guadalupe River near Gonzales.

The 43-mile section between San Marcos and Luling has three dams and at least a couple of rapids that can cause trouble if care is not exercised. (See map.) There is another small dam, the Rio Vista, just about a mile from the concrete launching ramp provided in the City Park in San Marcos. This one can be run by the adventurous about a third of the way out from the left bank. Take a look first; you may decide to portage left.

IH 35 crosses the river within the city of San Marcos about a half mile below the park. Unless the water level is low, some pipeline crossings just past IH 35 will necessitate a short portage on the left. The portages that are nearly always required along this portion of the San Marcos are a good reason to travel light with a minimum of gear. Another road crosses about a half mile past the IH 35

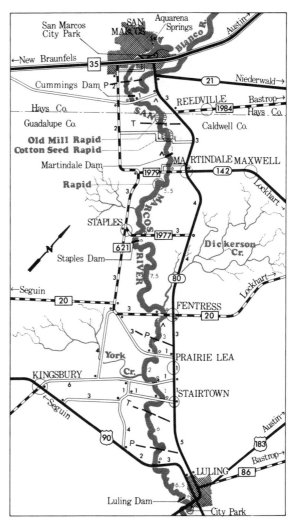

SAN MARCOS RIVER
San Marcos to Luling
43 Miles

crossing. The Blanco River joins the San Marcos 2.5 miles farther down from this point. Should either river be at a high level, there will be a strong whirlpool to the right at the point where the two rivers join.

A mile below this point is Cummings Dam; small yet dangerous, so portage to the right. A half mile past the dam is a county road crossing between SH 80 and FM 621, sometimes referred to as the Westfield Crossing. Pecan Park, a private campground on the left just before you get to the Old Mill Rapids, has complete facilities including electricity and showers. The rapids themselves are not considered a serious hazard, but take a look anyway before you head through. However, another 2.5–3 miles downstream will get you to the Cotton Seed Rapid, and you definitely should scout this one before running it. If in doubt, you can portage to the right along the old concrete dam. The next road crossing is a county road off SH 80 about three-fourths mile below the rapids called Scull's Crossing. Another private park with limited camping facilities is located on the right just above the Martindale Dam. Again, this small dam is dangerous, and you should portage to the right. About a half mile below the dam is a low water bridge that will not offer enough clearance at anything above normal water level. Portage to the right if necessary to be on the safe side!

At the FM 1979 crossing at Martindale, there is about 100 yards of public shoreline along the right-of-way. This crossing is approximately one mile below the dam. The Goynes Canoe Livery and Shady Grove Campground (512/357-6125) is located here, a fine facility and a good source of river information. There is a small rapid about one mile down and the next road crossing is that of FM 1977, some 5.5 miles down. This crossing also has about 100 yards of shoreline along the right-of-way about one mile east of Staples on FM 621.

Still another dam, Staples Dam, is located a half mile below this crossing. It, too, is dangerous, so portage. The next road crossing is at FM 20 just west of Fentress with some 75 yards of shoreline along the right-of-way. A county road off SH 80 comes in to a private camp a half mile down-stream. Another county road crosses 2.5 miles down about one mile west of Prairie Lea. It's 2 miles to the next road crossing one mile north of Stairtown with about 30 yards of shoreline along the right-of-way here. Another river mile gets you to still another county road crossing just east of Stairtown with 100 yards of shoreline available. A roadside park and 100 yards of shoreline are available at the US 90 crossing 6 more miles downriver.

The Luling Dam, another of the small but dangerous dams on the San Marcos, is 6.5 miles below the US 90 crossing and a half mile above the US 80 crossing just west of Luling. Portage to the right at the dam. The Luling City Park is located another half mile past the US 80 crossing. A half mile of shoreline and camping facilities are available here.

The 39-mile section of the San Marcos River from Luling to Gonzales where it unites with the Guadalupe River is also fine for recreational use except during periods of extreme drought. However, the banks are steep and muddy in places and log jams can present a problem. The best bet for camping is at the commercial private camps.

It is 4 miles from the Luling City Park adjacent to SH 80 just east of the city limits to the crossing of IH 10. There is no access to the river at this point. Different sources give different estimates of the distance from this point to the Ottine Dam, vary-

Rental canoes make river running affordable and accessible to anyone interested in trying this popular sport.

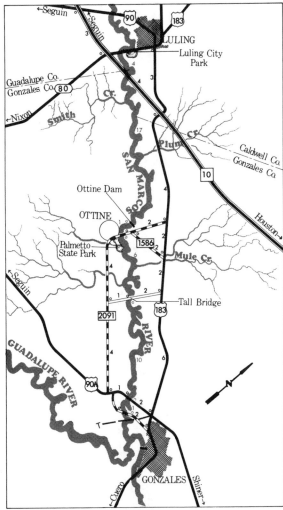

SAN MARCOS RIVER
Luling City Park To Gonzales
39 Miles

ing from 8 miles to as much as 17 miles. Be on the lookout for the dam and portage right. FM 2091 crosses about one mile below the dam near the town of Ottine. The banks are very steep here at this crossing making access difficult. The Palmetto State Park is just below this crossing and offers possible access at the abandoned low-water crossing in the park.

A county road off US 183, some 6 miles northwest of Gonzales crosses the river with a tall bridge another 6 miles downstream. The banks are steep and access from the bridge is fenced off. However, there is reportedly access offered at a low-water crossing at this point. US 90A crosses 10 miles downriver at a point 2 miles west of Gonzales. The banks here are also extremely steep. A county road known as the Old River Road crosses a mile below at a point some 2 miles above the junction of the San Marcos with the Guadalupe River.

Should you wish to continue your trip on down the Guadalupe to Independence Park in Gonzales or the US 183 crossing south of town, watch for the Gonzales Dam about 2.5 miles past the junction of the rivers. It is extremely dangerous especially at high water levels. Do not try to run it; take out well above the dam and portage to the right.

The Luling City Park, Palmetto State Park, and Independence Park in Gonzales offer the best camping opportunities for this section of the river. The facilities are limited, but adequate at these parks.

The San Marcos is truly a beautiful stream for the canoeist and should be on the "must" list for all who wish a bit of excitement along with a chance to "get away from it all!"

There is a carrier available for any-size group ready to tackle lake, river, or stream.

San Saba River

The San Saba River is another scenic Hill Country stream, beginning in the springs near the Schleicher-Menard County line. It flows about 100 miles to the east to join with the Colorado River east of San Saba. The area is predominantly ranch country and is relatively undeveloped and natural with no impoundments other than low-water crossings. This, too, is top whitetail deer country!

The 29-mile section from the headwaters near Fort McKavett down to the crossing of FM 2092 below Menard is narrow and shallow during normal water levels; during periods of high water, there are a few areas of swift water and some small rapids. There are two historical sites located along the banks in this portion, Fort McKavett and the San Saba Presidio.

Fort McKavett is an old army post that was built for the protection of the early settlers about 1852. Abandoned in 1859, the fort was re-occupied for a short time during the Civil War. General Ranald S. MacKenzie occupied the fort from 1868 to 1883 during the Indian campaigns. The fort is now a state historic park.

The San Saba Presidio which is located across the river from Menard is one of the early forts of the Spanish mission era. It was built in 1757, but the mission, located a few miles downstream, was very susceptible to surprise Indian raids. The mission was destroyed by Comanches in 1758, and the Spanish abandoned the presidio about ten years later. The rock ruins now on the site are the efforts at reconstruction of the fort by the citizens of Menard in 1936, the year of the Texas Centennial.

Even though this section of the river passes through a very scenic area with both historical and geological interest, its potential as a recreational waterway is limited by an insufficient flow. Still, the features of this section will be given with this bit of advice: Be forewarned that much of the river is very shallow.

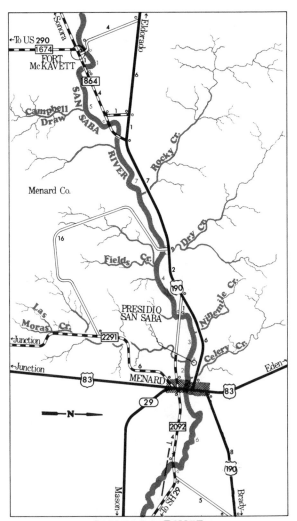

SAN SABA RIVER
Ft. McKavett to FM 2092
29 Miles

A county road off FM 864 just outside Fort McKavett makes a low water crossing that is fenced on all four sides where the river is very narrow and shallow. FM 864 crosses east of Fort McKavett about a mile downstream. It crosses again about 5 miles further down and again at another mile downriver. At last report, access at both of these points was fenced off. The first good access point is at the county road crossing off SH 29 some 8 miles west of Menard. The banks are low here as the river narrows from about 60 feet wide to 10 feet, and it is shallow. Another county road crossing off SH 29 some 4 miles west of Menard finds the river narrow and with the possibility of log jams, but the water upstream is clear and deep with recreational use possible. There are some high limestone bluffs in this section.

The San Saba Presidio is located on the left bank of the river one mile west of Menard on the munic-

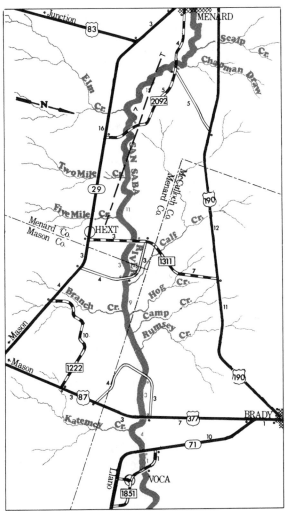

SAN SABA RIVER
FM 2092 To Voca Crossing
46 Miles

trude. Access is no problem as there are several road crossings. Even a slight rise in the water level should make this a very interesting float.

There is a private camp 10 miles below the FM 2092 crossing with camping facilities available. FM 2092 crosses again about 10 miles east of Menard. The river narrows again and is passable beneath the bridge. There is good access here with adequate parking space. FM 1311 crosses 3 miles north of the Hext community, but the crossing is fenced off on all sides. There is an old low-water crossing just upstream from this one. Three miles further downstream is a road crossing, but according to latest reports it is a private road. Another road crosses about 8 miles south of Brady and makes a loop between US 87-377, but it, too, is possibly a

The importance of waterproofing and tying in all gear cannot be stressed enough. This is true even for a day trip over calm water.

ipal golf course. A small road outside of the entrance provides access to the river. US 83 crosses in the city of Menard with a city park located beneath the high bridge on the flood plain. There is a low-water crossing just downstream from the park with good access, but the river is still shallow. Five miles east of Menard, FM 2092 crosses with good access and plenty of available parking space. With grassy banks and pecan groves, the river is wide upstream and narrow downstream, but at normal levels, it is passable beneath the bridge.

The 46-mile portion of the San Saba from the FM 2092 crossing down to the Voca crossing flows through Menard, Mason, and McCulloch counties, typical Hill Country terrain. The river will vary from 20 to 50 feet in width and is relatively shallow during normal levels. However, several rapids exist, and in places, large limestone boulders pro-

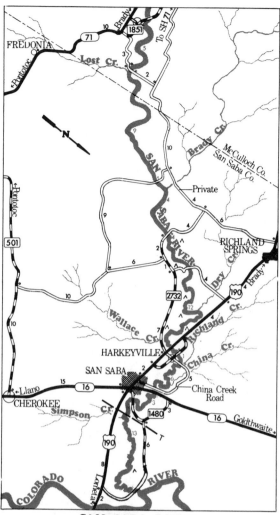

SAN SABA RIVER
Voca Crossing to Colorado River
59 Miles

private crossing. At the US 87-377 crossing 8 miles south of Brady, there is a roadside park just downstream from the high bridge with good access. The river is fairly shallow. The Voca crossing off FM 1851 offers poor access although the river here is some 50 feet wide.

From the Voca crossing to the Colorado River is a 59-mile section of the San Saba located in McCulloch and San Saba Counties that offers the most potential for recreational use during normal water levels. That portion above US 190 has crystal clear water and limestone outcroppings, but past the highway, the banks are steeper and the river gradually becomes muddy. That upper section also has a few small rapids, but there are none below US 190. There are many road crossings and several private camps along the way, so access to the river is no problem except at the high bridges from US 190 to the Colorado River.

Some of the road crossings are private with the surrounding land being privately owned as well, so ask before using any of the shoreline. Most of the private camps mentioned earlier do offer considerable shoreline access, but most of them do not have any facilities for the camper. The river passes within about one mile of the town of San Saba and enters the Colorado River approximately 15 miles downstream. There is a private camp about 2 miles upstream from the junction with the river with about a half mile of shoreline available, but no facilities are provided.

Here, a "rubber duckie," a homemade raft or one of poor quality, is offset by a well-prepared family in a sturdy rubber raft, with each member in a properly fitted life jacket.

Sulphur River

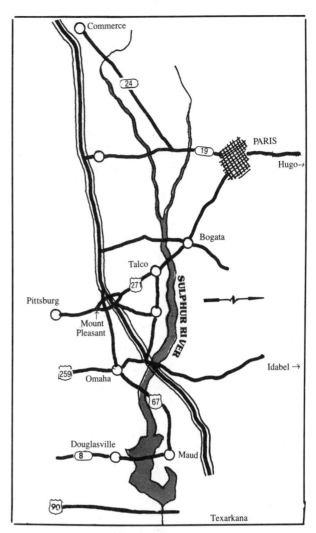

SULPHUR RIVER
Lake Wright Patman Dam to Hwy. 59

With approximately 75 miles of waterway within the state of Texas, the Sulphur River's main claim to fame is perhaps the fact that Lake Wright Patman, formally known as Lake Texarkana, was formed from it by the dam southwest of Texarkana. The Sulphur flows into the Red River some 15 miles into Arkansas. It begins in Delta County where the North and South forks come together and flows very slowly through heavy timberland. Due to much channelization upstream, the water here is usually on the muddy side, but there is normally enough of it for recreational use. Although that portion of the river below the dam has much higher-quality water, it depends on the release of water from the dam as to whether it can offer more than very limited recreational use. The section close to the crossing of US 59 is very popular for fishing both from the bank and from boats.

There are several access points to the river: the US 259 crossing between De Kalb and Omaha, the US 67 crossing where a public boat ramp is maintained by the Texas Parks and Wildlife Department, and the SH 8 crossing between Maud and Douglasville. Here the lake begins. There is also a TPWD boat ramp located at the US 59 crossing be-

low the dam. There are no further road crossings between this point and the Texas-Arkansas state line some 17 miles downstream.

Many rivers are easily accessible through Texas Parks and Wildlife Department boat ramps, such as this one.

Trinity River

The four forks of the Trinity, East, Elm, West and Clear, come together and flow some 550 miles to the Gulf with a volume of 5.8 million acre-feet that is exceeded only by that of the Neches and the Sabine. The Trinity gets its name from the Spanish "Trinidad." Alonso de Leon named it "La Santisima Trinidad," the Most Holy Trinity. The lower course of the river was developed for navigation until around the turn of the century.

In addition to the Ray Roberts Lake and Lake Lewisville on the Elm Fork, there are four reservoirs above Fort Worth: Lake Worth, Eagle Mountain, and Bridgeport on the West Fork, and Lake Benbrook on the Clear Fork. There are two other lakes on the Clear Fork before it joins with the main stream, Lake Lavon and Lake Ray Hubbard. The Trinity has within its drainage area more large cities and population and greater industrial development than any other river basin in Texas. Perhaps this is one of the reasons that the upper portions of the river have gained the reputation of being rather highly polluted. However, much has been done in recent years to "clean up" the river, and the water quality becomes increasingly better as it moves downstream.

From its beginning near Saint Jo in Montague County, the Elm Fork of the Trinity River flows some 85 miles to the southeast to unite with the West Fork to form the main stream of the Trinity. Lake Dallas was built on this stream in the mid-twenties. It was later enlarged and renamed the Garza-Little Elm Reservoir. After another enlargement and name change, it is now known as Lake Lewisville.

The portions most suitable for outdoor recreation are the eight-mile stretch between the Ray Roberts Dam and the headwaters of Lake Lewisville, and the 22-mile stretch below the Lake Lewisville Dam down to just below the SH 114 crossing at the California Crossing Park. Launching points are provided below the Ray Roberts Dam

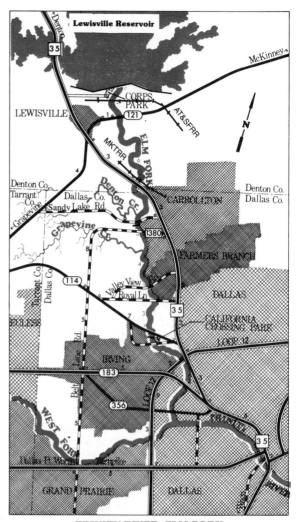

TRINITY RIVER, ELM FORK
Lewisville Reservoir to
California Crossing Park
22 Miles

and at the major highway crossings upstream of Lake Lewisville. Launch below that lake at the Corps of Engineers Park immediately below the dam, or if the water level should happen to be too low, at the SH 121 crossing just over a mile downstream. There is reportedly good access on both sides of the IH 35 crossing, but because of the usually heavy traffic, I personally try not to use the Interstate crossings.

About 3 miles past the IH 35 crossing is the Sandy Lake Road crossing and the Carrollton dam. Do not try to run the small dam at either low or high levels; always portage on the east bank. The park here at this crossing makes a good takeout point for a day's float. At the last report, no overnight camping is allowed at either this park or at the California Crossing Park.

Belt Line Road or FM 1380 crosses the river about one-half mile below the dam in the western city limit of Carrollton. The next crossing is at Valley View Road in the western city limit of Farmers Branch another 4 miles downriver. Other crossings include Royal Lane in the southwestern city limit of Farmers Branch at 2.5 miles, and the SH 114 another 3 miles in the northwestern city limits of Dallas. Another small dam is located just below this crossing and a portage is necessary. The California Crossing Park is adjacent to the dam on the east bank. This is a good takeout point, but the river can be floated on down to the junction with the West Fork and finally to the main stream of the Trinity.

While this portion of the Elm Fork normally has enough water flow for recreational use, it does flow through a heavily populated metropolitan area. And although the Dallas municipal water authorities try to keep the stream open, log jams are sometimes a problem since the river course lies through areas with heavy growth of elm, oak, and willow. A timely inquiry of one of the many canoe rental services in the Dallas-Fort Worth area will give you up-to-date information on the river.

The section of the river from the point where the Elm and West forks come together down to the crossing of SH 7 between Crockett and Centerville covers some 230 miles. Characterized by steep muddy banks lined with cottonwood, elm, sycamore, and willow, recreational use is still rather limited due in part to the reputation from past years of being highly polluted by Fort Worth and Dallas.

The 33-mile section of the river from SH 7 to SH 21 is perhaps the first portion of the river that is extremely well suited for recreational use. While I would certainly not recommend drinking the water right out of the river, I recently crossed on SH 21 and the water looked great! There are lots of sand bars along this stretch that are suitable for day use and camping. Access at SH 7 is a bit difficult due to the steep banks, but there is a boat ramp and large parking area at the SH 21 crossing. However, the Commissioner's Court has prohibited overnight camping.

The river along this section is now wide enough to eliminate the problem of downed trees blocking the stream, a problem common to some of the smaller streams that flow through the piney woods of East Texas. Incidentally, if you are using a powerboat, this SH 21 crossing is a good launch point for a run either up or down stream.

The next 44-mile section of the Trinity is the boundary between Madison and Houston counties and after flowing through about 15 miles of Walker County becomes the boundary between

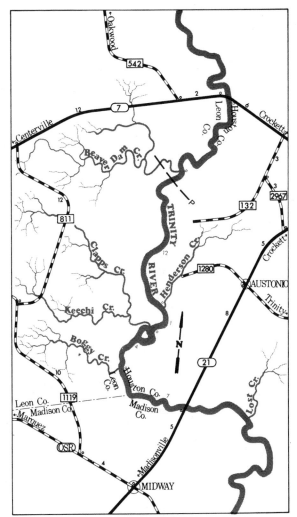

TRINITY RIVER
SH 7 to SH 21
33 Miles

Walker and Trinity counties. Although the banks are often steep and muddy, there are the usual sand bars available for camping and day use. Several large creeks (see map) enter the river along this section and offer opportunities for a bit of exploration for the canoeist or small-boat traveler.

There are no road crossings between the SH 21 and the SH 19 crossings some 6 miles southwest of Trinity. There is a small boat ramp here. For the last 4 miles of this section, the water begins to back up behind Lake Livingston. This 90,000-acre impoundment is a popular fishing and recreational area and offers outstanding facilities.

The 32-mile section beginning immediately below the dam offers an excellent float with high quality water depending on the amount of water being released from the lake. There is a minimum flow at all times that is sufficient for most uses. The best source of information on river flow is the Trinity River Authority at 713/365-2292.

The Dam Site Marina just below the dam off FM 1988 on the left bank has a ramp for launching and a parking lot, but there is a small fee. This portion of the river has the reputation of being one of the best spots for white bass fishing in the entire state. It should be noted that the first 1,000 feet below the dam is a closed area due to the fact that there were 17 confirmed drownings during the first 6 months of 1982 in this tailrace area. There are fences along the shoreline and an overhead cable with signs across the channel. In addition to the white bass, this has been a popular spot for catfish and striped bass. You're also likely to see huge alligator gar rolling on the surface as you proceed down the river.

Down the river 11 miles is the US 59 crossing with some 150 yards of shoreline in the right-of-way, but the access is rather difficult at times. From the dam to here makes a fine day float for the canoeist or small-boat user. You will likely see signs of many trotlines being used by fishermen all along the lower portion of the Trinity. I like to set out a line or two myself, especially when camping overnight on a river, but be sure to check the latest Texas Freshwater Fishing Guide brochure from the Texas Parks and Wildlife Department for the current regulations. It is available wherever licenses are sold. Don't be in too much of a hurry; you will want to enjoy all the river has to offer.

Netting was completely banned in Houston and Madison counties above Lake Livingston in September of 1980 in order to protect the concentrations of both white and striped bass that move up-river to spawn. This no-net regulation is also for

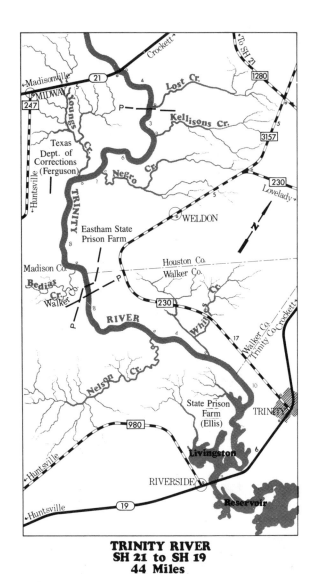

TRINITY RIVER
SH 21 to SH 19
44 Miles

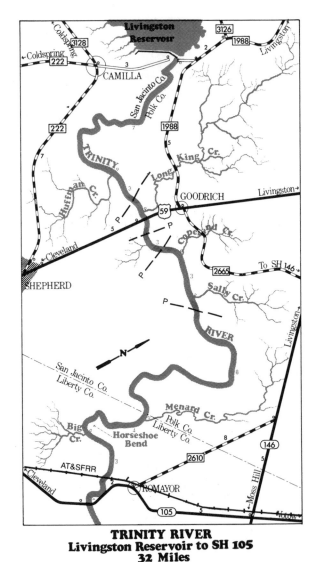

TRINITY RIVER
Livingston Reservoir to SH 105
32 Miles

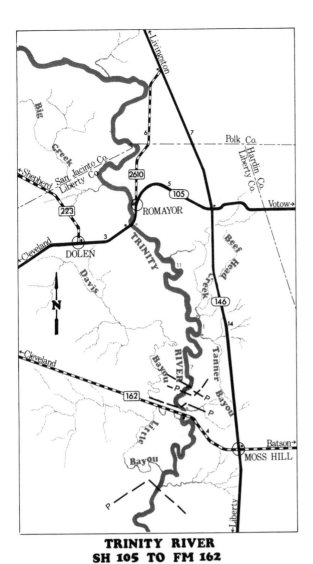

**TRINITY RIVER
SH 105 TO FM 162
19 Miles**

sand bars in the more remote areas that have so far escaped the developers.

The avid fisherman might want to inquire at Romayor about the old gravel pit fishing holes here. Not too far from the banks of the Trinity, good management has produced some fine fishing for bass, catfish, and various sunfish.

The 29-mile section from the FM 162 crossing to Liberty and the US 90-SH 146 crossing is all within Liberty County and through what used to be considered a part of the Big Thicket. This area has also been invaded by the developers, but there are still sections that are unchanged from the days when those who wanted to could "disappear" into the Thicket to escape the law or the problems of civilization.

Because water from the Trinity is used for irrigating downstream rice fields during the growing

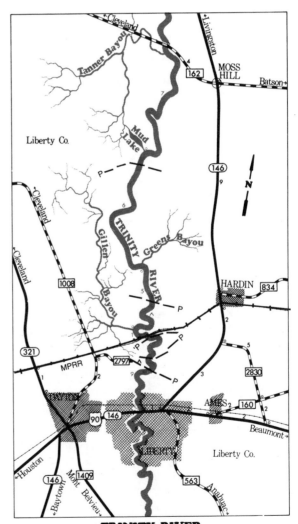

**TRINITY RIVER
FM 162 to Liberty
29 Miles**

the protection of the easily netted flathead or opelousas catfish.

The next river crossing is 21 miles down to the SH 105 bridge where access is also a bit of a problem for larger boats. There is about 100 yards of shoreline available here. This section of the river flows through both timbered and cultivated land, as well as some developing sub-divisions. Still, there is plenty of the "natural state" left with sand bars for both day and overnight camping. Be sure to get permission before using any banks that are private property.

From this SH 105 crossing near Romayor to the FM 162 crossing between Cleveland and Moss Hill is a 19-mile scenic stretch through natural hardwood bottomlands that has several housing developments along the river. Just stay on the river through these and confine your camping to the

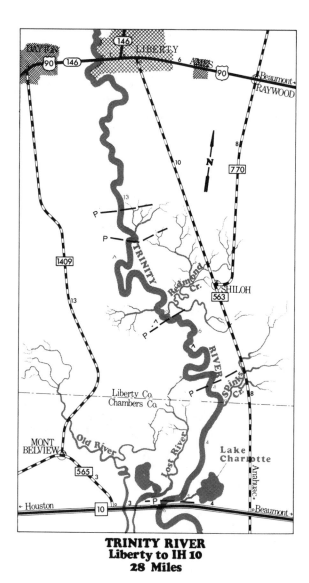

TRINITY RIVER
Liberty to IH 10
28 Miles

The section of the Trinity below Liberty holds some very special memories for me. When I was just a teen-ager, my favorite uncle lived in Liberty, and my older brother and I would sometimes get to spend as much as a week at a time there. My uncle would take us out to a fish camp owned by a friend of his, an old Frenchman, who would try to work us to death running his bait traps and trotlines! He kept us going day and night, and we loved every minute of it! We would seine more sand bars and bait more trotlines in a week than we normally would get to do in a year.

We ate plenty of fish, too. Mr. Arceneaux's wife would come out from town every day or so and bring a big pan of cornbread. He preferred the freshwater drum or gaspergou to catfish, and to this day, I, too, had rather have a gou to eat.

The old man kept a parrot for company, and that bird thought he was head of the family. His vocabulary consisted of three words: "Hurry right back!" It made no difference to him that you may have just arrived or had been there all day; he would still loudly tell you to "Hurry right back!"

The shoreline of this 28-mile section of the Trinity from Liberty to the IH 10 crossing between Beaumont and Houston gradually becomes more swamp-like and marshy, but the river channel remains well defined. There are some private camps located along the way with boat ramps, but as always, get advance permission before using any private facility or property.

While I do not recommend it except for the most experienced, it is possible to explore the large sloughs and bayous that feed the main stream. One of these near the county line (see map) links the river with the so-called Lost River. One could explore the Lost River-Old River system and then rejoin the Trinity about 2 or 3 miles below IH 10. The Chambers County Highway Map available from the state would be invaluable for anyone wanting to make such a float.

Good access to the river reportedly is provided along the right-of-way of IH 10. From this point, it is another 8 miles to where the river enters Trinity Bay. Refer to that Chambers County Map for help in navigating the several channels that form. Both wind and strong tides can be a problem here in this lower section.

One could conceivably spend a lifetime along the full reach of the Trinity River. The tremendous variety of its environment and wildlife just might make such a commitment worthwhile.

season, there is an almost continuous release of water from Lake Livingston, and thus there is ample water for recreational purposes, too.

Tanner Bayou and Mud Lake join the river some 7 miles below the FM 162 crossing. Normally there is enough water here to allow exploration of this scenic area. An important checkpoint for determining your position on the river is the railroad bridge 4 miles southwest of Hardin. It is 19 miles from FM 162 and 9.5 miles upstream from the US 90-SH 146 crossing in Liberty.

About 5 miles below this railroad bridge is a private camp off FM 2797 that has a boat ramp. A second railroad bridge is 4 miles downstream and just above the highway crossing. A boat ramp is available at this point in Liberty.

Village Creek

If only I had been wearing ear plugs, I could have imagined myself way back in the "boonies" with no sign of civilization for miles and miles! My introduction to Village Creek was a photographic assignment for a story on the Big Thicket for one of the major outdoor magazines. All alone, I unloaded my canoe at the US 287-69 crossing just south of Village Mills. Barely out of sight of the highway bridge, but certainly not out of hearing, the plant and animal life so characteristic of the Big Thicket completely enveloped me!

Like the TV commercial that says, "You can't eat just one!" you can't get by with just one visit to this remarkable area. Before you begin a float on the creek, I'd suggest a visit to the Big Thicket National Preserve Visitor Station located about 4 miles east of the highway on FM 420. No matter how familiar you may be with the area, you'll learn something new and interesting about the plant and animal life of the "Thicket" plus some of the history and legends that combine to make it an exciting experience!

Although there is usually enough water for the trip just about any time of the year, the heat, the humidity, and the insects during the summer months can diminish the fun and turn an extended float into hard work. An in-and-out trip like that first one of mine can be O.K., but for a through-trip, I'd try to pick a cooler time. I've also heard some pretty tall tales about the size of the snakes that live here, but I've not found them to be any larger or meaner than any of the ones on Texas streams that flow through swampy-type bottomlands. Just keep your eyes open and exercise the usual precautions when in snake country.

Another suggestion for a pre-float activity is a visit to the Big Thicket Museum at Saratoga on FM 770. The museum offers guided canoe trips within the Thicket that are an excellent way to be introduced both to the area and to canoeing.

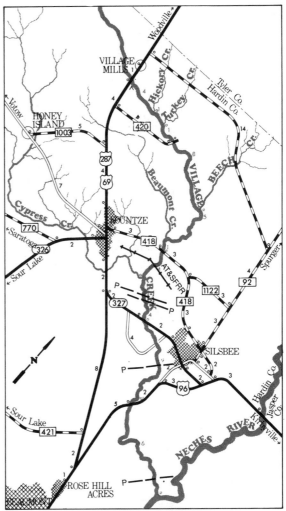

VILLAGE CREEK
US 69 & US 287 to US 96
37 Miles

The first section of Village Creek usable for floating stretches approximately 19 miles from the US 287-69 crossing to FM 418. There is easy access to the creek at both crossings. Much of the land is owned by Kirby Lumber Company and is reportedly open to the public. However, due to the increased leasing of timber lands to hunting clubs, it is always best to make a few local inquiries to make sure that use of the shoreline is still permitted. There is reportedly about 2 miles of shoreline on the right bank that is open for use.

About 6 miles below the US 287-69 crossing, FM 420 crosses the creek near the Big Thicket National Preserve Visitor Station. There are four large creeks, three from the left and one from the right, (see map) that enter the main stream. This section can be covered in a long day of paddling, but it makes an ideal overnight float with camping on

The camaraderie of group camping is the very essence of being out-of-doors, and the cooking chores are shared by all.

one of the sand and gravel bars. Don't try to be "tough;" use an insect-snake-proof tent!

The next section from FM 418 to the US 96 crossing south of Silsbee is about 17 miles and makes a fine overnight float, or it can be divided into two short trips by either launching or taking out at the SH 327 crossing near the mid-point. From FM 418 to SH 327 is 8 miles; from SH 327 to US 96 is 9 miles. There is about 200 yards of shoreline available at this mid-point with a TPWD boat ramp at the US 96 crossing. As a reference point or emer-

gency takeout, there is a county road that crosses the creek a couple of miles below SH 327.

Village Creek joins with the Neches River about 6 miles below the US 96 crossing at a point some 15 miles below where the Neches crosses US 96 near Evadale.

Due to the very delicate balance of nature in this area and the fact that a lot of it is to be included in the Big Thicket National Preserve, always remember to leave your campsites cleaner than you found them!

A well-planned canoe trip helps insure the success of the venture. Many times canoeists must carry everything needed for the trip including drinking water.

Wichita River

One of the principal tributaries of the Red River, the Wichita River flows for some 90 miles through Archer, Wichita, and Clay counties. Two impoundments, Lake Kemp and Diversion Reservoir, are located on the river, and the recreational use of the river between them normally depends on the water releases from Lake Kemp dam. Although the river is not usually classed among the most scenic of the state, it does represent an important recreational resource to this area.

Either during the early spring or late fall, the 46-mile section of the river between Diversion Dam and Farm Road 369 near Wichita Falls is an interesting float provided enough water is being released. The river flows between sand and caliche banks with many sand bars in the river bed. Quicksand, though sometimes found, is not usually the problem that it can be on the Red River.

There is a 10-mile section of the river above Lake Kemp after the North and South forks come together that normally has enough water for recreational use. Back-up water from the lake adds to this making that portion immediately above the lake almost always suitable. The 14-mile portion between Lake Kemp and Diversion Reservoir depends on water releases from the Lake Kemp Dam.

If sufficient water is being released, the section of the river west of the city of Wichita Falls offers an unhurried trip that may include some shallow water. There are no commercial campsites, but most floaters prefer to use natural ones anyway. Access to the river is available at several locations: the county road crossing just below Diversion Dam, the FM 1180 crossing, the SH 25 crossing, the FM 368 crossing, and the FM 369 crossing.

The section of the river from here through the city and on to the Red River, although not mapped here, can afford recreational floats when it is on a

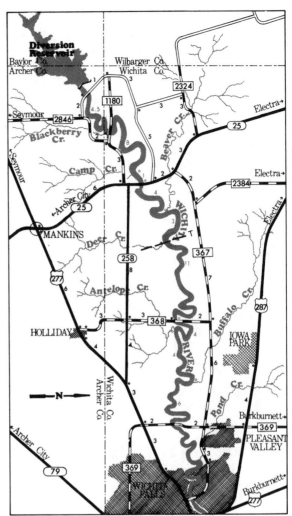

WICHITA RIVER
Diversion Dam to FM 369
46 Miles

rise after heavy rains or if the release from the upstream dams is sufficient. The city of Wichita Falls was named after a 5-foot waterfall on the river, but time and floods have since washed it away.

As we conclude the listing of the major rivers and streams in Texas, perhaps some of your favorites have been omitted. The chances are they will be listed in the next section on what I refer to as the secondary streams. Even this listing will not be complete since the Texas Almanac states that some 3,700 streams are identified in the *U.S. Geological Survey Gazetteer of Texas Streams*. If you still fail to find them, it could be a cause to be thankful; the chances are that you'll have that favorite all to yourself!

SECONDARY STREAMS AND WATERWAYS

The saying that "big is not necessarily better" certainly applies to many of the smaller creeks and rivers of Texas. Depending, of course, on what you wish to do, I would say that the recreational opportunities offered by some of the lesser streams in that list of 3,700 might even exceed that of the "biggies."

I've parked the camper beside some of them and enjoyed a peace and quiet that I haven't found around the busier waterways. I've walked the banks of some (with the landowner's permission, of course) too small to offer boating or canoeing and caught a fine stringer of creek bass. I grew up on the banks of a little year-round creek that flows along the back side of our old home place. It'll take me a long time to ever equal the fun that I had there or to catch as many little catfish and bream as that stream produced.

I'm even going to list that one in this section on the secondary streams so no one can accuse me of holding out on my favorites. I own about a mile of shoreline on one side of it, so if you want to climb its banks, you're welcome, but see me first!

Because there are so many of them, these smaller rivers have probably given more people more hours of recreation than some of the larger, better known rivers. I have listed here in alphabetical order, 46 of these smaller and seasonal streams that you may have overlooked. I've an idea that as you check these, you'll discover others not listed here that can give you many hours or days of fun and recreation. Just remember that "big may not be better, but little can be leisure at its best!"

Aransas River

The Aransas River does contain sufficient water for limited recreational use from a county road crossing east of Skidmore in Bee County to the public boat ramp on FM 629 in Refugio County. The river is the boundary between San Patricio and Refugio counties and empties into Copano Bay on the Gulf just southwest of the Bayside Community. US 77 crosses the river between Refugio and Sinton for additional access to the river. Portions of the stream may be as much as 100 feet wide as it meanders through typical coastal prairie land.

Armand Bayou

The bayou is unique in that it represents an unspoiled area of vegetation that includes palmettoes, oaks, Spanish moss, cattails, and flowering water plants close to the Houston metropolitan area. Much of it lies within the city limits of Pasadena in the southeastern part of Harris County. It is joined by Big Island Slough and Horsepen Bayou to form an area known as Mud Lake, and then flows on into Clear Lake just east of the Lyndon B. Johnson Space Center. How long it can remain a scenic natural bayou will depend on the local development in this high-use area. The average width of the bayou is about 40 feet, widening into a poorly defined marsh in some areas.

Arroyo Colorado

This stream is located in Cameron County and flows through the southern edge of the city of Harlingen on its way to the Laguna Madre on the Gulf. The lower portion from FM 106 in Rio Hondo down to Arroyo City near the Laguna Madre is normally suitable for recreational use. As with many of these lower coastal prairie streams, very little current will be noticed. The Texas Parks and Wildlife Department maintains a boat ramp at this FM 106 crossing and at the FM 1847 crossing near Arroyo City.

Austin Bayou

Located in Brazoria County east of Lake Jackson, this bayou offers an important recreational resource to local residents although its use is seasonal. It is rather narrow with only a limited flow of water, but there is said to be a 10-mile portion in the vicinity of FM 2004 that has potential for recreational use. It flows into Bastrop Bayou which will be covered later.

Barton Creek

From its point of origin in the western part of Travis County, the creek flows about 35 miles to enter the Colorado River below Lake Austin and above Town Lake. Although it is an intermittent stream, during periods of heavy rainfall, it is considered by some to be a fine white-water experience. Like any stream that depends on a fast rise, it should be considered very dangerous for all but those with plenty of experience with white water. During these periods of high water, access can be had from a road off FM 2244 just south of Westlake Hills to that portion of the creek that flows through Zilker Park in Austin. Loop 360 crosses the creek about a mile northwest of its intersection with US 71. The park is located on Bee Caves Road inside the Austin city limits.

Bastrop Bayou

Like its neighbor, Austin Bayou, this typical scenic coastal waterway offers some 20 miles of bayou flowing deep enough for recreational use most of the time. A Parks and Wildlife Department boat ramp at the FM 2004 crossing northeast of Lake Jackson in Brazoria County provides convenient access. Austin Bayou joins with this one as it flows on into Bastrop Bay and the Intracoastal Canal.

Bedias Creek

This creek forms the boundary line between Madison and Walker counties between Madisonville and Huntsville. The section between US 75 southeast of Madisonville and the Trinity River has the greatest potential for recreationists, especially during periods of high water. Log and brush jams even then can be a problem. The creek is 20 to 50 feet wide with a series of long pools and short riffles. There is one rapid that takes about a 10-foot drop in a 50-foot stream distance, so be on the lookout for it! Also during the periods of high water in the upper portions of the creek, the main channel is sometimes hard to pick. FM 247 crosses the creek about half way between US 75 and the Trinity River. A graded dirt road off FM 247 goes down to the point where the creek joins the river.

Beech Creek

The upper section of this spring-fed creek in Tyler County has been designated as one of the streams in the "String of Pearls" concept of the Big

Thicket National Park. This part is north of Spurger and south of B. A. Steinhagen Lake on the Neches River. While it is an unpolluted stream with cool water and white sand bars, its course through a heavily timbered area means that it is subject to many log and brush jams. For one willing to put up with such problems, the 23-mile section from the FM 1013 crossing in Tyler County to its junction with Village Creek in Hardin County is suitable for float trips during periods of above normal water level. The last 4 miles above Village Creek is probably the best section for recreational use during normal water levels, and it can be reached by traveling about 8 miles over a county road off US 287-69 east of Village Mills.

Big Cow Creek

With headwaters in the northwest corner of Newton County, it winds and twists southeasterly through the county for about 90 miles to its junction with the Sabine River southeast of Call. Fed by many spring branches along its course, it travels first through an area of rolling sandhills, open mixed forests, and pine groves. The lower section is mostly through bottomland hardwoods and pine. Probably the best section for recreational use begins at the crossing of SH 87 about 2 miles southwest of Newton. Other road crossings between here and the Sabine River include FM 363, FM 2460 at the Singletary Sites, and FM 1416. A county road goes in to the river just below the point where the creek joins the river. The water flow on this lower section is usually sufficient for most recreational uses.

Big Cypress Creek

The creek begins in northwestern Tyler County and flows some 25 miles to unite with Turkey Creek. It was also one of the proposed areas for the "String of Pearls" concept of the Big Thicket National Park, but for some reason was not selected. However, it does flow through some beautiful and primitive countryside, and although the water level will vary, most of the time there is enough for recreational use. Log and brush jams do make the creek a difficult float. Probably the best section to try is an 18-mile stretch from a county road crossing off FM 256 about 6 miles west of Woodville to the crossing of US 287-69 just south of Hillister. This creek then unites with Turkey Creek just north of the point where FM 1943 crosses Turkey Creek. FM 1943 marks the northern boundary of the Turkey Creek Unit of the Big Thicket National Park.

Big Mineral Creek

Located in Grayson County, the North and South branches of the creek unite just north of Whitesboro and flow into the Big Mineral arm of Lake Texoma on the Hagerman National Wildlife Refuge. It flows through thick woodlands and is seldom over 50 feet wide at any given point until it reaches the lake area. Picnic tables, grills, and restrooms are available in the refuge, and access to the creek is no problem within the refuge itself. A 1.5-mile section of the creek was once proposed for marking as a canoe trail by the refuge, but no information is available as to whether this was ever done. Check it out if you're in that area.

Big Pine Creek

This one flows across the northwest corner of Red River County through farming and ranching country with an occasional stretch through bottomland hardwoods. While the creek may range in width from 30 to 45 feet, the best section for recreational use is a 5-mile run from the crossing of FM 410 to the crossing on the Red River of SH 37. The creek runs into the Red about a mile above this crossing.

Big Sandy Creek

With its headwaters to the east of the Seven Oaks community in Polk County, Big Sandy Creek flows for some 40 miles through the heart of the Big Thicket. It passes through the Alabama-Coushatta Indian Reservation between Livingston and Woodville, and one of the public campgrounds operated by the Reservation is located on the creek at the US 190 crossing. Located along the creek and just below the Indian Reservation is the Big Sandy Creek Unit of the Big Thicket National Park. FM 1276 passes through this Unit and over the creek. This road again crosses the creek about .6 mile before joining FM 943. FM 943 runs somewhat parallel to the creek as it flows on into Hardin County to unite with Village Creek west of Village Mills on US 287-69. The creek becomes deeper after passing through the Reservation and steep banks are present at most of the road crossings. Look for a lot of brush and log jams unless the water level is somewhat above normal.

The start of a race on Buffalo Bayou is the invitation to spills for some and thrills for all.

Bois D'Arc Creek

One of the major drainages of the Red River in Texas, Bois D'Arc Creek flows from near Whitewright in Grayson County southeasterly into Fannin County. From the SH 11 crossing east of Randolph, the stream has apparently been channelized as it flows northeasterly past the city of Bonham until it reaches a point where the Thomas Branch joins the stream about 4 miles east of Lake Bonham. After being crossed by a county road and FM 1396, it takes a more northerly direction into the Caddo National Grassland where it seems again to have been channelized into a straight ditch. FM 100 crosses at a point between portions of the Grassland, and the creek flows in its natural course to cross FM 79 about 2 miles before entering the Red River. There is normally enough water on this 2-mile stretch for recreational use, but the nearest road crossing on the Red River below here is US 271 some 40 miles away. Most of the time, the water in the creek is clear and the fishing is good. Good camping areas are available where the creek passes through the Caddo National Grasslands which are administered by the U.S. Forest Service.

Buffalo Bayou

Beginning in the north central section of Fort Bend County, this well-known bayou flows for some 65 miles southeasterly into Harris County where it forms a part of the Houston Ship Channel, eventually emptying into Galveston Bay. Even though parts of it have become extremely polluted in the past, it is floatable most of the time. Since it flows through Houston, there are numerous access points, but the best section is said to be that between SH 6 and Loop 610.

Caney Creek

Caney Creek forms just south of US 82 west of Bonham between the towns of Ector and Savoy in Fannin County. The crossing of FM 1753 west of Ravenna marks the beginning of recreational possibilities, and there is usually an adequate water level most of the year. The creek flows between a few high bluffs and rocks. The short segment between the low water crossing of a county road between FM 1753 and FM 3321 (off FM 274) and the Red River is the most feasible for recreational use. The next downstream crossing of the Red is that of SH 78.

Catfish Creek

Ranging in width from 15 to 45 feet, Catfish Creek is located in the northwest corner of Anderson County where it flows through the Gus Engling Wildlife Management Area and then through the Coffield State Prison Farm. It has retained much of its natural character as it flows through typical East Texas bottomlands. While its entire length is suitable for some kind of recreational use, overhanging willows and submerged logs can be a problem, especially during the dry season. Camping facilities are available at several unimproved, public campgrounds on the Wildlife Management Area. The most favorable stretch of the creek is from the crossing of FM 321 down to the intersection with the Trinity River and down the Trinity to the US 84 crossing.

Cedar Bayou

This is another typical coastal bayou that offers quite a bit of recreational potential even though there is considerable development along its shores. Beginning in northeastern Harris County, it forms the boundary between Harris and Liberty counties and also between Harris and Chambers counties, emptying into Galveston Bay south of Baytown. The estuary at its mouth is said to be an important spawning area for fish, shrimp, and oysters with the entire area serving as a winter feeding and nesting area for ducks, geese, and other aquatic birds. Approximately 40 miles of the lower bayou is said to be satisfactory for recreational use.

Cibolo Creek

Although it is one of the longer streams in the section of the state north of San Antonio, Cibolo Creek is often dry in too many areas to be suitable for normal waterway recreational activities except during periods of consistently rainy weather. Its 96 miles are contained in Kendall, Bexar, Comal, Guadalupe, Wilson, and Karnes counties with baldcypress trees lining its banks to its junction with the San Antonio River about 3 miles north of Karnes City. Near the headwaters of the creek in the vicinity of the crossing of US 87 southeast of Boerne, there are reported to be two unique vegetative and geologic areas—Cascade Cavern and Honey Comb Rock (inquire locally for more complete information). The average flow of water in the creek is reportedly about 30 cubic feet per second which is not enough for normal waterway use.

Clear Creek

This creek forms the boundary between Harris and Brazoria counties as well as that between Harris and Galveston counties. Said to be an extremely scenic waterway as it passes through heavily vegetated shores, the lower 12 to 15 miles are perhaps the best suited for recreational use. One of the best sections is between the TPWL boat ramp in the Galveston County Park and the FM 528 crossing in Friendswood.

Coffee Mill Creek

Located in the northeast portion of Fannin County, this rather short stream flows eastward into Coffee Mill Lake in the Caddo National Grasslands. The 2.5-mile section from just west of the FM 2029 crossing on to the lake is suitable for recreational use almost year round. Campsites are plentiful within the National Grasslands.

Coleto Creek

Formed by the junction of Fifteenmile Creek and Twelvemile Creek on the boundary between Goliad and Victoria counties, Coleto Creek is their common boundary before turning eastward into Victoria County to unite with the Guadalupe River south of the city of Victoria. It is a beautiful sandy creek with that section between the FM 622 crossing on the county line and US 77 being suitable for recreational use during periods of abundant rainfall. Other crossings include US 59 and FM 446.

See *A Guide to Fishing in Texas,* Lone Star Books, Houston, Texas, for information on the new Coleto Creek Reservoir.

Comal River

Although it has the distinction of being the shortest river in Texas, only 2.5 miles long, it is a highly utilized river as it flows through the city of New Braunfels. Because of the input of Comal Springs which have the largest flow of any springs in the state—an average of 303 cubic feet per second—the waterway is reportedly suitable for most types of recreational use almost year round. The river joins the Guadalupe River within the city of New Braunfels.

Denton Creek

This stream is located in the northeast corner of Tarrant County and the northwest corner of Dallas County with a short swing into the southern edge of Denton County. The lower 6 miles below Grapevine Reservoir are said to be a favorite section for recreational use. The water level is normally fairly low with a slow current. The creek is usable when the flow ranges from around 60 cubic feet per second up to about 300 cubic feet per second. At the higher rate of flow, there are some rapids. Submerged logs can be a problem at the lower rate, and overhanging limbs may cause a bit of a bother. Access to the creek is available through the Grapevine Recreation Area off FM 2499 or SH 26 or SH 121. The creek flows into the Elm Fork of the Trinity River west of Carrollton, and the Sandy Lake Road crosses the Elm Fork just below the junction.

Canoeists enjoy a lazy day on a slow-moving creek.

Dickinson Bayou

With headwaters in eastern Brazoria County near the town of Alvin, Dickinson Bayou flows eastward into Galveston County and Dickinson Bay, a small section of Galveston Bay. Only 20 miles long, the upper section likely has insufficient flow for recreational use. There is a scenic 13.5-mile stretch from the Cemetery Road off FM 517 down to the crossing of SH 146 about a mile and a half before it enters Dickinson Bay. A Texas Parks and Wildlife Department boat ramp is located on this portion at the crossing of SH 3. This is a typical, slow-moving coastal bayou.

Double Bayou, East Fork

This is a scenic, winding waterway located in Chambers County on the east side of Trinity Bay and about half way between Lake Anahuac and East Bay in Galveston County. The last 7 miles from the crossing of FM 562 to the entrance to Trinity Bay is suitable for recreational use, but access to the bay is rather difficult in this area. By shortening the float to about 4 miles, there is access to a paved road east of Oak Island. That 4-mile segment offers a good way to spend about 2½ hours. Portions of the upper reaches of the bayou that extend on north of IH 10 are also suitable for use.

Garcitas Creek

Located in the eastern portion of Victoria County, Garcitas Creek becomes the boundary between Victoria and Jackson counties for about the last 10 miles before it enters Lavaca Bay. FM 616 crosses the creek near La Salle with a TPWD boat ramp located here. There is a 6-mile stretch of still water from this point to Lavaca Bay, but there are no access roads at the mouth of the creek.

Highlands Bayou

This is another one of the bayous of Galveston County, flowing just south of La Marque into Jones Bay. Its still waters offer a potentially good section for recreational use from SH 6 to FM 2004. Depending upon your energy and speed, this section could offer as much as a 3–4 hour float.

Keechi Creek

The East and West forks of Keechi Creek combine in the northeastern part of Palo Pinto County to make this tributary of the Brazos River. SH 254 crosses the creek just east of Graford, and the section of the creek from here to the crossing of SH 337 is suitable for recreational use during periods of heavy rainfall. The creek then flows into the Brazos River about 2 miles below this crossing. The next crossing of the Brazos is that of FM 4 north of Palo Pinto. Keechi Creek flows through the rough, rugged country of the Palo Pinto Mountains.

Lake Charlotte Creek

Also known as Lake Pass, this 2–3-mile section between Lake Charlotte and the Trinity River is located on the northern edge of Chambers County about 3 or 4 miles north of IH 10. During those periods of sufficient rainfall when the creek is suitable for recreational use, it can be reached either from the river or through the lake by way of a paved road off FM 563 near the county line.

Little Cypress Bayou

Sometimes referred to as Little Cypress Creek, it flows across the northern portion of Upshur County and into the northwestern part of Harrison County. It continues on to become a part of the boundary between Harrison and Marion counties before it runs into Big Cypress Bayou east of the city of Jefferson and west of Caddo Lake. Portions of the upper reaches, possibly as far up as the crossing of SH 155 in Upshur County, may be usable for some forms of recreation, but due to the fact that it flows through heavily timbered wilderness-like areas, many log jams make floating a problem. However, a float from the crossing of US 59 south of Jefferson on into Big Cypress Bayou and Caddo Lake should be possible. A lot of wildlife can normally be seen in this area also.

Navasota River

Although much longer than most of the secondary streams listed, much of the 125 miles of the Navasota River does not have sufficient flow for recreational use except during periods of consistently rainy weather. From its beginning in the southeastern part of Hill County, it flows through Limestone County where two small and one large reservoirs have been built. Lake Mexia is located west of the city of Mexia and the Fort Parker State Park Lake is approximately 8 miles downstream. There are two smaller low-water dams located at one mile intervals below the park. A new and much larger reservoir, Lake Limestone, has been built on the Navasota River, the dam itself being in Robertson and Leon counties.

The river continues on its way to join the Brazos, forming the boundary line between Robertson and Leon counties, Madison and Brazos counties, and Grimes and Brazos counties. As it flows through dense hardwood forest areas, log jams are just one of the problems found. As the river nears its junction with the Brazos, the flow increases making recreational use more feasible. The lakes on the river do offer a lot; see *A Guide to Fishing in Texas* (Lone Star Books, Houston, Texas) for information on them.

Onion Creek

Located in Travis County south of the city of Austin, the creek flows in a northeasterly direction to unite with the Colorado River east of Del Valle. McKinney Falls and the McKinney Falls State Park are located on the creek southwest of Bergstrom Air Force Base. It is suitable for some forms of recreation provided above normal water conditions exist. Floaters will encounter a number of easy rapids in addition to the falls, depending on the water level.

This girl epitomizes the spirit of river recreation—wet and fun!

Oyster Bayou

Another of the coastal bayous that offers opportunities for recreational use, Oyster Bayou lies in Chambers County with that portion from FM 1985 down to East Bay always having a sufficient but slow moving flow and about a 100-foot width. The bayou passes along the east boundary of the Anahuac National Wildlife Refuge, and many species of waterfowl can be seen. Nutria are plentiful as are alligators. Also, the refuge is said to be one of the last remaining strongholds of the endangered red wolf. A dirt road on the refuge goes almost to the mouth of the bayou at East Bay. This one is an excellent example of a fine coastal bayou.

Oyster Creek

This one has potential as a recreational waterway from the crossing of SH 35 west of Angleton in Brazoria County through the city of Lake Jackson to the crossing of FM 523 east of Freeport. The creek flows through a heavily populated region on its way to the Gulf of Mexico. The above mentioned stretch of the creek is about 25 miles long.

Palo Pinto Creek

Palo Pinto Creek in Palo Pinto County flows through the mountains by the same name to join with the Brazos River near the little town of Brazos. A section suitable for recreational use is located between the SH 108 crossing near Mingus and Palo Pinto Reservoir. Also that portion below the reservoir down to the crossing of FM 129 south of Brazos is usable. While the upper section is suitable practically the year round, the portion below the dam depends on the amount of water being released.

Pecan Bayou

Beginning in Callahan County, the bayou flows to the southeast through the northeastern corner of Coleman County, across Brown County to join the Colorado River in Mills County. With a length of about 100 miles, it has the distinction of being the farthest west of any stream carrying the name "bayou." Its recreational use depends on periods of heavy rainfall, especially in the upper sections. Lake Brownwood is on the bayou and it is an excellent recreational lake. (Check *A Guide to Fishing in Texas*, Lone Star Books, Houston, Texas, for information on this fine lake.) Reportedly, a good section for recreational use when the water level is sufficient is that between SH 206 near Burkett in

Coleman County down to FM 2559 above Lake Brownwood.

Richland Creek

Said to be one of the larger creeks in Texas, it rises in Navarro County southwest of Corsicana and flows easterly on through the north corner of Freestone County where it enters the Trinity River just south of the crossing of US 287 between Corsicana and Palestine. One of the favored sections is that between the FM 709 crossing south of Corsicana and the US 75-IH 45 crossing just north of the Richland community. During above normal water levels, there are a couple of rapids just below a county road crossing about 3 miles below the FM 709 crossing that can be exciting! The lower portions of the creek could be worth looking into on a local basis since it is a big creek. Log jams can be quite a problem all along the creek. Should you go on into the Trinity River, it is a long, long way downstream to the next crossing, that of US 84-79.

Sanders Creek

Located in Lamar County, this creek flows into the Pat Mayse Reservoir and then from below the dam on into the Red River. The backwaters of the lake extend almost to the crossing of FM 1499 within the Pat Mayse State Wildlife Management Area. There is a 3–4-mile section here that can offer some recreational use. Pat Mayse State Park is along the north shore of the lake just above the dam. When water is being released from the reservoir, there is a possible 4–5-mile stretch from the dam to the Red River just above the crossing of US 271. The creek is from 30 to 45 feet wide flowing through bottomland, hardwood, and farm land.

Sabinal River

Rising in the southwest corner of Bandera County, the Sabinal flows through the eastern side of Uvalde County to join with the Frio River down in the southeastern corner. With a total length of about 58 miles, it does pass through some very scenic portions of the Hill Country including picturesque Sabinal Canyon. After it passes from the Edwards Plateau in Uvalde County, it mostly flows underground during normal water levels. However, during times of heavy rainfall, the upper portions of the river have a good potential for recreational use. Local information may be secured from either Vanderpool, Utopia, or Sabinal.

Salado Creek

This is a clear, spring-fed stream that flows into the Lampasas River in Bell County just above where the Lampasas and Leon rivers combine to form Little River. The area offers such things as mineral outcrops, unusual geological formations, Indian camps, and historic sites. The creek flows through the town of Salado, famous for its Stagecoach Inn. While the creek must be on a rise before there is sufficient water for any extensive use, the portion between FM 2843 and FM 1123 does contain some excellent white water during periods of heavy rainfall. The creek flows through the cross timbers and rolling prairies of this portion of central Texas.

San Jacinto River, East Fork

The East Fork of the San Jacinto River is formed in San Jacinto County within the Sam Houston National Forest and flows southeastward through the northeast corner of Liberty County. It touches a small portion of Montgomery County and flows on into Harris County where it joins the West Fork and Lake Houston. The East Fork is extremely narrow and much smaller than the West Fork. Normally it does not have enough water flow for recreational use, although, with permission from private landowners or within the National Forest, I have had fun walking the banks and fishing. During or following heavy rains, some portions can be used for floats, but log jams and overhanging limbs are always a problem. Check its big neighboring impounds, Lake Livingston, Lake Conroe, and Lake Houston, in *A Guide To Fishing in Texas*, (Lone Star Books, Houston, Texas).

Spring Creek

Flowing through an area of mixed hardwoods and pines, Spring Creek forms the boundary between Montgomery and Harris counties and joins the West Fork of the San Jacinto River within the city limits of Humble. The section between IH 45 and US 59 is the most suitable for recreational use, and is good except during periods of exceptionally dry weather. It is fairly narrow and log jams can be a problem.

Taylor Bayou

Taylor Bayou meanders through scenic tree-lined banks in the central section of Jefferson

County as it flows into Sabine Lake at the southwest corner of Port Arthur. A county road crossing off SH 73 some 7 or 8 miles west of Port Arthur offers access to the bayou as does the SH 73 crossing at the edge of Port Arthur where a TPWD boat ramp is available. There is an abundance of wildlife in the area, especially waterfowl as it passes just north of the J. D. Murphree Wildlife Management Area. A TPWD boat ramp is also available here.

Turkey Creek

From its point of origin just north of Woodville in Tyler County, the creek flows southward through Woodville and on into Hardin County to its junction with Village Creek southeast of Village Mills. As one of the connecting corridors in the "String of Pearls" concept of the Big Thicket National Park, the Turkey Creek Unit extends from the crossing of FM 1943 in Tyler County all the way down to FM 420. This lower portion includes the junction of Turkey and Village creeks. The National Park Service has a visitor center on FM 420. Some clearing of the channel is to be done along with the creation of hiking trails along the creek.

Straw Creek

Last and maybe least, out of order alphabetically anyway, I just had to wind up with this one even though you have to know where it is to even find it on the Shelby County Highway Map. It is there however! I list it because it was on this little creek that I "cut my teeth" on creek fishing. As I mentioned earlier in this section on the secondary streams, Straw Creek is the eastern boundary of my dad's place where I grew up, and I now own a considerable length of one side of it. I caught my first fish on a rod and reel, a beautiful little bass, just below one of the pools. My son caught his first bluegill while sitting with me on a log across it. Although it is sort of filled in now, we once had a great swimmin' hole in a big bend where a deep hole had been scoured out by heavy rains. My dad, my older brother, and I made a lot of tracks along its banks putting out set hooks for catfish. Our record catch was somewhere in the 6-pound class, but to me, it was a monster!

If you really want to find it, look just east of the Neuville, Choice, and Clever Creek communities in the south-central part of Shelby County. Fed by a spring branch that flows the year round, I've never known old Straw Creek to stop running.

I sort of hope I can be like that, 'cause I never want to stop "runnin'" our Texas rivers and streams!

Sometimes the most enjoyment of a creek comes not from a float or fishing, but from merely sitting on its banks.

Index